MARGARET MITCHELL

Margaret Mitchell (November 8, 1900-August 16, 1949) spent her girlhood and young ladyhood in the home of her father, which stood here. Her family had lived in Atlanta since the city's earliest days. She was born and lived in Atlanta all her life.

After her marriage to John Robert Marsh (July 4, 1925), she wrote *Gone With the Wind* over a period of ten years—1926-36—while residing at 979 Crescent Ave., NE (1925-32) and at 4 17th St., NE (1932-39).

She was a reporter on the *Atlanta Journal* for four years (1922-26).

She died on August 16, 1949, from an accident suffered near here.

Her novel, which was published June 30, 1936, has been translated into 25 foreign languages.

GEORGIA   HISTORICAL   COMMISSION

I REMEMBER MARGARET MITCHELL

I REMEMBER

MARGARET MITCHELL

by

Yolande Gwinn

COPPLE HOUSE BOOKS, INC.
Lakemont, Georgia 30552

Manufactured in the United States of America

DEDICATION

This book is dedicated to my late parents, James and Marypearl Copley Gwin, and to the memory of Margaret Mitchell.

ACKNOWLEDGEMENTS

With much love and affection to Patsy Wiggins. Also, deep appreciation and many thanks to my many friends who provided me with their memories of Margaret Mitchell.

Publisher's Note

Except for the Prologue and the articles reprinted by permission of the original publishers, we have endeavored to put the letters, which constitute material not before printed, in a chronological order according to the writer's association with Margaret Mitchell. This was not completely successful, but that pattern prevails.

Likewise, the picture sections, except those which illustrate reprinted material, are also arranged as nearly as possilbe in a chronological fashion. The first picture section represents the pre-book era, the next, the book and movie era, and then the post-book era of Margaret Mitchell and *Gone With The Wind*.

We also gave careful consideration to the grammar, spelling and punctuation of material quoted — letters and reprinted material. Except for obvious typos, we did not edit the letters or material. Each retains the flavor of its writer. That is not to say we did not miss some typos when we proofread our typesetting. If you find a few, forgive us. Very few books are perfect in the first edition. *Gone With The Wind*, for such a long book, had only two, which is a remarkable record.

Our credit page is simple. We have listed the fact that permission was granted *carte blanche* for reprinted material and pictures used with a simple listing, except in rare cases where a credit line was requested. We are grateful for this simplification.

Why another book about Margaret Mitchell? It is doubtful that any new material about Margaret Mitchell will surface. These letters from Margaret's friends and her letters to them give us additional insight into the kind of person she was. A person we wish we had known.

Many, many people claimed they knew Margaret Mitchell, when, in fact, they did not. We feel Yolande Gwin, a remarkable lady, deserves a bit of applause for gathering and putting together this material from friends of Peggy, as they called her, who *really* knew Margaret Mitchell.

PROLOGUE

It was hot and humid in Atlanta on the night of Aug. 11, 1949.
The mercury had hit 92 degrees in the afternoon and there was a sticky feeling in the atmosphere.

Families, all in scanty summer attire, were riding around the city amid what they supposed was the "cool of the evening". Young lovers, oblivious of the heat, were concerned only with themselves and the moonlight. Others sat around public, private or club pools or on front porch swings. The patio had not emerged as a household word.

Some, with an eye toward civic affairs, discussed the lead editorial in the paper that day. It said, in part, "realizing the liquor controversy to be one widely discussed, and the industry to be one which provides legal control, and realizing, also, the legal industry to be one which supplies the state some $8,000,000 (eight million) in taxes instead of allowing illegal operators to receive all the profits, we intend to keep the issue factually before the public to the best of our ability."

Others talked about Herbert Hoover, the only living former president, who had, the previous day, celebrated his 75th birthday in Palo Alto, California. In a speech, he made it known that "government spending and taxes threaten the nation with collectivism".

On the entertainment level, some radio die-hards had stayed at home and listened to dance musical programs by Wayne King, Guy Lombardo and Lawrence Welk, and those with an appetite for suspense, tuned in to "Counterspy." TV had not matured nor gathered the strength to clutch and hold in its grip more than half of the American public.

At the Rhodes Theater at Rhodes Center on Peachtree Street, *Gone With the Wind* had just completed a run. The picture Atlanta claimed, and still does, as its very own, was on the neighborhood circuit in Atlanta and as well in many cities throughout the nation. At another theater, located on the very same Peachtree Street which had been immortalized by GONE WITH THE WIND, there was the homey neighborhood atmosphere and feeling. Yet, this theater, The Peachtree Arts, was different. Its program showings were first runs of foreign films.

On this hot August night, it was no exception. The movie, *A Canterbury Tale* with Eric Partman and Kim Hunter, was rolling to the delight of many who had waited outside in line to see the film. The last show was scheduled at 9:30 p.m.

13

The picture had received good reviews, and some of the night workers around Atlanta thought it would have been fun to see it. But there had to be many compromises in many cases, for when duty calls, there must be an answer.

One of these was a young intern at Grady Memorial Hospital named Edwin Lochridge Jr. He was blaming only himself for being a "shut-in" that night except when he rode the ambulance for accident calls — all because he was substituting for an intern pal who wanted the night off.

Mrs. John R. Marsh was at her apartment on South Prado at Piedmont Avenue. She had complained that she did not feel well, a statement other women have made since Eve. She had rested that afternoon and did not dress for dinner; she and Mr. Marsh always enjoyed their enclosed glass dining room. Mrs. Marsh recalled that the movie, A Canterbury Tale had been recommended. Perhaps attending the movie would revive her spirits.

So, they decided to go, and Peggy Mitchell dressed.

Nothing happened to delay Margaret Mitchell's rendezvous with death that evening. Fate moved with accuracy and timelike precision. No obstacles stood in the path to the movie. The chain of events which led to the fatal accident was unbroken. Every moment was synchronized with the stopwatch of destiny.

The usual trivial things which accompany a casual departure of a husband and wife for a movie did not happen — like forgetting to lock the back door, looking for the car keys, taking the last look into the mirror. Any of these things would have desynchronized the deadly chronometer.

Everything worked hand in hand with fate as the couple drove through the tree bordered winding streets of Ansley Park toward Peachtree Street. Mrs. Marsh was driving. She had been the driver for her husband, Georgia Power Company executive Marsh, due to his "ailing" after several heart murmurs.

The couple continued southward on Peachtree. Even the traffic lights played into the hand of fate — all were green-on go. None had the stop-red signal. So here again the synchronization went unbroken.

The Peachtree Arts Theater was — and still is — on the east side of Peachtree Street between 13 and 14th streets. Mr. and Mrs. Marsh heading South, found a parking place on the west side of Peachtree in a vacant lot, just below the 13th street intersection. (Thirteenth street dead ends at Peachtree.) Parking spaces were plentiful. There were no parking meters nor "1 hour" parking signs. The couple left their car and started across Peachtree on the crosswalk.

Fate, grinning on the sideline, watched an automobile roaring out Peachtree northward. Passersby, some going to the movie, others just walking along content with their own thoughts and dreams, hardly noticed the little woman and her tall heavyset companion.

But they would have gasped, looked and even begged for an autograph had they known her identity — the famous author of *Gone With the Wind* — and also the little celebrity who shunned publicity.

So, with her husband holding her by the arm, Margaret Mitchell Marsh began her last walk across the street she had made famous. It was approximately 9:18 p.m. They wanted to get a good seat before the late show at 9:30 p.m.

In the words of John Marsh, "We had started across the street in a hole in the traffic, the instant when no cars were passing either south or northward. I am not as strong as I was before I had a heart attack a few years ago and we always made a practice of waiting for these holes in traffic before attempting to cross a busy street."

"Peggy was on my left side as we crossed the street," Mr. Marsh reported after the accident. "I was between her and the approaching car. That may have influenced the split-second decisions we both made, mine to go forward, hers to go backward. There was no consultation between us nor time for it. Maybe not being able to see the car as well as I, she leaped back to get a better view.

"Whatever the reason, she tried to make it back to the curb we had just left. And I am confident she would have made it, if the automobile had not gone into that long deadly skid that swung it further and further in the same direction she was going as if it was chasing her down.

"If it had skidded toward the east side of the street instead of the west, it probably would have gotten me, not her. This was certainly an accident that did not have to happen. If Peggy had been given even one more second of time, I think she would have made it."

So, the little woman with the worldwide fame jumped back into a cave of destiny, to disappear slowly but surely into the enveloping mists of time and history.

The car which took to the point of no return, first dragged her fragile little body 15 feet. At the death wheel was a 29-year-old taxi driver operating his own private cab/car.

Somewhere in the back of the crowd which quickly gathered around the little creature, was Fate, chalking up another perfect time record. John Marsh rushed to the side of his wife, bruised and unconscious. There was a protective circle around the two, and someone ran to the theater to call an ambulance.

Intern Edwin Lochridge, Jr., at Grady, deeply engrossed in a magazine story, got the emergency signal. In routine manner, he grabbed his bag, climbed in beside the driver and headed toward another traffic call.

The screaming siren pierced the calmness of the summer evening and the two riders shared the same thought — another poor soul is hurt and is dying or is already dead. When the ambulance arrived at Peachtree and Thirteenth Street, what the two found was not pleasant. A woman had been knocked down, she had an injury to her left leg, was bruised and life- less, but breathing.

"It was dark of course," recalled Lochridge. "When we arrived many people had gathered around her. I did not recognize her in the dark."

Her body was lifted by hands as gentle as a mother's and placed on a stretcher and slipped into the ambulance. John Marsh rode with the driver and Intern Lochridge sat in the back beside her battered body. Again, with sirens screaming the big red ambulance sped towards Grady Hospital, the famous city hospital named for the famed orator of the South, Atlanta's own Henry W. Grady.

When the body of Margaret Mitchell was removed from the ambulance and rolled toward the X-ray room where there was plenty of light, and only then, with horror, did he realize it was Margaret Mitchell.

"As soon as I could I rushed to a telephone to call my parents," said Lochridge, now a prominent practicing physician in Atlanta. "Mother came down the next morning. As she was out when I called, my father broke the news the next morning." Mrs. Lochridge came down to the hospital the next morning to help with the many calls that were flooding the switchboard. The whole world knew by then of the terrible tragedy.

Hugh D. Gravitt, the 29-year-old taxi cab driver whose private automobile struck down Miss Mitchell paid a visit to Grady Hospital in an attempt to visit the injured author. He went to the hospital with his wife several hours after he paid $5,450 in bonds on charges growing out of the mishap.

Friends of Miss Mitchell were always staying at the hospital to help out in any way. Some of these friends said Mr. Gravitt expressed deep concern over Miss Mitchell's condition. John R. Marsh, husband of Miss Mitchell, told an *Atlanta Journal* reporter that Gravitt had phoned him at his home.

"I haven't spoken to him and I don't intend to talk to him," said Mr. Marsh.

Mr. Marsh explained that friends at Grady Hospital had furnished to Gravitt his (Marsh's) phone number when Gravitt and his wife went by Grady to inquire into Miss Mitchell's condition.

Among those present in the information room where Mrs. Durden presided were Mrs. Edwin Lochridge, Mrs. George Eubanks, Jr., Mrs. Wright Bryan, Miss Kate Edwards and Miss Marguerite Steadman.

After the death of Miss Mitchell there was only one link remaining with the hospital and Miss Mitchell's death there. Nancy Wooten was the nurse who was in charge of Miss Mitchell. Mrs. Wooten retired from the hospital in June 1980.

However, she says she vividly remembers bringing in ice from the ice house behind the hospital for the novelist's oxygen tent.

As the days passed, Margaret Mitchell seemed to be winning her private battle, as Atlanta doctors at Grady Hospital said that she was "slightly improved".

She was taken to the hospital Thursday night, and doctors suspected her skull was fractured.

Friday night Miss Mitchell had partically regained consciousness. She drank a glass of water and rallied a bit to say she "hurt all over".

She recognized members of her family and delighted them by answering coherently, but was still suffering from shock, according to her brother, Stephens Mitchell, who added that she was speaking very low.

The news of her accident made news all over the nation and overseas. U.S. President Harry Truman sent her a telegram saying, "Hope you are better soon."

Friday evening her temperature dropped to one hundred and one degrees. It had been two or three degrees higher during the day.

Miss Mitchell could not be removed from her hospital room for X-rays. Doctors suspected her skull was fractured.

A sudden sinking spell hit a bit after 11 a.m. All attendants were alarmed.

Three doctors were with her at the time of her death, namely Dr. W.C. Waters, Dr. Charles Dowman and Dr. Exum Walker. Also present was Mrs. Carrie Lou Reynolds Mitchell, her sister-in-law. Miss Mitchell's brother, Stephens Mitchell, had just left the room. Several of Miss Mitchell's friends were at Grady Hospital that morning. They soon became aware of the situation within the room nearby.

These friends continued to answer the phone and told callers that the situation was critical, but their tears told the story.

Frank Wilson, superintendent of the hospital, was in constant attendance. Mrs. Louise Durden, P.R. Director of the hospital, was equally alert and attentive.

Miss Mitchell never regained full consciousness. She had been in a coma since the accident.

Shortly after noon, Dr. Waters and Stephens Mitchell left the hospital to tell John Marsh of his loss.

Then Atlanta, the state and the nation knew what had happened.

"I knew Margaret Mitchell" was the cry. The contents of this book are from her many friends who really KNEW HER.

"I knew Margaret Mitchell" was the cry. The contents of this book are from her many friends who *really* knew her. . .

TURMAN SISTERS

*Two Atlanta sisters, Mrs. Edwin Lochridge (the former Lethea Turman)
and Mrs. Morris Markey, (the former Helen Turman) have many memories of
their friendship with Peggy Mitchell.*

*The Turman sisters grew up in the family home in Hexagon Hall in the
Lakewood area of Atlanta.*

Mrs. Lochridge recalled how Peggy would come out to their
home and sit fascinated over the many stories their mother, the late
Mrs. S.B. Turman and her mother, the late Mrs. John Miller Clarke
Reed, would tell about the Confederate veterans and the War
Between The States and how they had to leave Atlanta when it was
burning, thanks to General Sherman.

Their grandfather told them to climb into an open carriage and
head for Macon, Ga., and he would meet them there. As they drove
southward, and to their horror and sorrow their home had been
burned to the ground. Nothing was left but the cabins where the
servants lived and the barn. This beautiful home was at the corner of
McDonough Road and Lakewood Avenue on the outskirts of
Atlanta. This handsome and beautiful home was a six sided structure.

GAUSE

Mrs. E. Barton Gause is the former Laura Rose and graduated from Washington Seminary with other members of the 1918 class — among the graduates was Margaret Mitchell.

"We, Peggy and I, walked to school every morning for five years. We lived within a block of each other near Peachtree and 17th street.

"We would meet each school morning at Pershing Point and then walk to school. (It was located just south of Brookwood Rail Station.)

"When I finally made it to the senior class, the family gave me a car."

During the years she and Peggy walked, with them was another Seminary student, Elizabeth Shewmake, who is now Mrs. Thomas McCleskey who lived on West Peachtree Street opposite 11th Street.

Editor's Note: Mrs. Gause said they never took a lunch from home to school.

"No, we would all go over to the kitchen (of the Seminary Boarding School) and there was Theodore, the kind old black man who made sandwiches for all the students.

In the class prophecy, she was acclaimed to become an aviator."

MERIWETHER

Mrs. Charles Meriwether, is the former Elizabeth Little of Atlanta and has many happy memories of Margaret Mitchell.

She was always so clever and delightful and a real companion in small groups but never in large ones. Back in our highschool days a lot of us would get together and stage plays in various homes. Margaret wrote all of them and acted as director. It was more fun and many times we would have the plays at the home of my uncle and aunt on Seventeenth Street. My memories of her are among my prize possessions.

AICHEL

Mrs. Aichel is now ninety years old and living in Jacksonville, Florida. She is a native of Atlanta.

About 1921, Louis and I (newly married), were asked to chaperone a group of young people on a house party at Mr. Victor Smith's farm at Buford, Georgia. Mr. Smith was a member of "North Avenue," and Louis was a long-time member of the Tech Bible Class at North Avenue, the connection, I suppose.

The only ones I remember there at the house party were the Turman girls, Lethea and Helen, and Margaret Mitchell. It was a fun time for all. However, Margaret Mitchell was the life of the party, unquestionably, and kept things lively. I cannot remember anything specific she said or did, and at that time I did not realize we had a celebrity in our midst. Nor did she, I'm sure. However, when I read *Gone With The Wind*, I remember remarking to my father, "Scarlett O'Hara is certainly the personification of Margaret Mitchell." To have known her for those brief few days was a worthwhile experience.

I do not remember the name of Margaret Mitchell's date there, but I do remember wondering why an attractive person like Margaret Mitchell could be interested in dating a person of so little personality.

Margaret Rosser Aichel (Mrs. Louis Aichel)

Washington Seminary graduating class of 1918. Margaret Mitchell is center front.

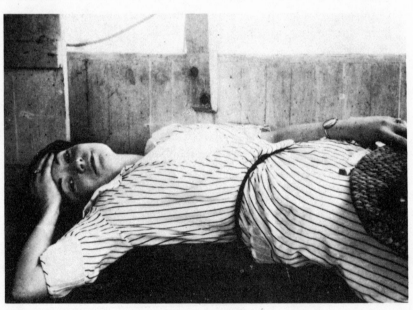

A moment of leisure at Smith College.

MARGARET MITCHELL

Margaret Mitchell and John Marsh were married July 4, 1925 and moved into a small apartment at the corner of Crescent Avenue and 10th Street. Margaret continued to work on the Atlanta Journal Magazine (now the Atlanta Weekly.) However, in 1926 she left the magazine, but after writing articles for it, she sprained the ankle she first had broken in childhood and later was seriously hurt by a fall from her horse. She was in a cast for weeks and remained in bed most of the time. Every afternoon John Marsh brought her books from the library.

This went on for weeks and weeks. Finally, one afternoon when he came home, minus the books, he had a large writing pad. He threw it on the bed and said:

"You have read everything I've brought you so now you write a book!"

So, taking his advice as always, she began to write her then to be famous book — Gone With the Wind.

She wrote the last chapter first as she started writing. As each chapter was finished, she stuffed it in large manila envelopes. Soon they were stacked almost to the ceiling of the apartment. She wrote and wrote much to John Marsh's pleasure.

The couple named their apartment "The Dump." On the door were two cards "Mr. John Marsh" and "Miss Margaret Mitchell." The neighbors were shocked. But it was 1925 and scandal was everywhere. But the Marshes were Mr. and Mrs. When guests were coming, including many members of the press, she had stacked the envelopes around the apartment living room, and she covered them up with blankets, coverlets and sheets.

When the book was published in 1936, their friends suddenly realized that they had been sitting on a masterpiece and didn't know it.

As time passed the Marshes moved to an apartment on 17th Street between the Peachtrees in 1932.

EASTMAN

Mrs. Edmund M. Eastman, the former Virginia Maude, was the daughter of the late Mr. and Mrs. Walter Maude who lived a little over one block south of the Eugene Mitchell home on Peachtree.

Peggy was writing her book at the time but never admitted it. She always loved to have friends come by on Sunday afternoons. It was so much fun and we were all having afternoon tea. She was a most gracious hostess and always drew people into conversations.

One time she said to me that she had cut a poem out of the paper. "I liked it so much that I cut it out and stuck it on my mirror in my bedroom. But I didn't notice until later that your mother wrote it!"

The poem titled Dixie was written by Mrs. Maude and appeared in 1932 in a book called Georgia Poets.
Mrs. Maude was the former Daisey Arnold of Atlanta.

Dixie

It seems a marvel when a simple strain,
Heard casually in cinema or street,
Awakens tremors of memorial pain
And conjurs vistas of sublime defeat.
It seems a marvel when the swelling chest
Resists the bondage of the censored will
When resonant, unbidden shouts invest
The silence with a quick and poignant thrill!

A stranger would not dream the simple score
Was fraught with power to sway a peaceful race,
To speed a nation on its march to death
This whimsy of a wandering troubadour!
He would have marveled had he seen them face
The shrapnel with the song upon their breath.

OWEN

Mrs. Sidney Owen remembers her mother, who was the late Mrs. S.R. Dull. Her famous cook book, titled Mrs. Dull's Cook Book, *is still a best seller.*

Mother wrote a column on foods and recipes for the *Atlanta Journal's Sunday Magazine*, (now the *Atlanta Weekly*). Mother wrote her column at home and sent it to the paper.

Peggy Mitchell was working at that time on the magazine and edited the copy. Mother always said Miss Mitchell was so nice to work with and even the two of them had telephone conversations.

Mother always said:

"She (Miss Mitchell) must have liked me for she never changed my copy."

Peggy used to send out cards at Christmas, the inside was nothing but this:
To announce the birth of Jesus Christ.

HUGER

Mrs. William E. Huger Sr., the former Sarah Orme, daughter of the late Mr. and Mrs. A.J. Orme, grew up on Peachtree and 13th Street, just a few blocks south of the Eugene Mitchell home.
Mrs. Huger remembers:

Peggy was older than I, but we became good friends playing and skating up and down Peachtree Street prior to our attending Washington Seminary. Atlanta's Private School for girls farther out Peachtree (then at I-85 intersection).

"Peggy tried always to do the right thing. Though she often became terribly upset over various situations at school, she never showed it nor complained. She certainly tried to be kind to our friends no matter what their attitude was toward her. But I do think she suffered a lot over "teen-age snobbishness" and her exclusion from several societies which would have made her high school life a lot happier. Many years later she related these disappointments in several talks with me.

"That she had a brillant mind is undoubted. After the Seminary, Peggy was accepted by and attended Smith College in North-hampton, Mass. In our day, girls from here (Atlanta) rarely attended such difficult Northern Institutions. Unfortunately, Peggy never finished Smith, as her mother died, so she came home to keep house for her father.

"Although our lives grew apart as time went, I would run into Margaret every so often. Even when she had become very famous, she never changed — she was always the warm, friendly girl who had grown up with all of us on Peachtree. Her success never went to her head at all."

LATHAM

Harold Latham of MacMillian Publishing Company in New York came marching through Georgia in 1935, his intentions were far better than another man from the North, William T. Sherman who burned down the city.

When Mr. Latham arrived in Atlanta he went to call upon Margaret Mitchell, at the suggestion of a mutual friend at the publishing company named Lois Cole. Miss Mitchell and her husband, John Marsh lived at No. 4 17th Street N.E. Apart. 9. (It was between Peachtree and West Peachtree Streets.) They had moved from their apartment, called "The Dump", where they lived after their marriage. It was on 10th Street at the corner of Crescent Avenue.

Latham told Miss Mitchell that Lois Cole had told him that Mrs. Marsh was writing a book and would she let him have it for future publication. Miss Mitchell refused by saying, "Oh. I haven't finished it!" "You have no title!" asked Latham. The answer was, "Yes, I have two. One is 'Tomorrow's Another Day' and the other is 'Another Day'." But Mrs. Marsh added that she had some others, but did not like them.

As Mr. Latham was leaving her to return to the Atlanta Biltmore Hotel where he had checked in that morning, he asked her once more if he could see the manuscript he had heard she was writing. "Oh, as I said before, I haven't finished it."

"Well," insisted Mr. Latham, "What is the title?" Her answer: "Tomorrow is Another Day."

He then left her apartment, got in a taxi and returned to the hotel. That evening he called again and asked for the manuscript. Her answer was "NO!"

Later that evening, either because of some inner voice or perhaps her husband's urging her to give Mr. Latham the book, she went to bed, perhaps to dream on the subject.

The next morning she piled all her written work in large manila envelopes, put them in the car, and drove to the Biltmore Hotel. She called Mr. Latham's room and he came right down to the lobby where she was sitting with the stack of envelopes hanging high over her head. "Take these before I change my mind!" she said. He grabbed them all and returned to his room. (Later he recalled in an interview, that he had to buy two large suitcases to pack in the manila envelopes.)

That evening, Miss Mitchell called the hotel to speak to Mr. Latham (she had changed her mind and wanted the copy back.) Mr. Latham had checked out and was gone with the wind to New Orleans, La. in his southern tour for book manuscripts.

Miss Mitchell returned to her apartment and sat down and tried to think of an appropriate title for her book, so she could wire it to Mr. Latham at his New York office.

As she thought of one title, she would write it down and start to think again, other than the title she had given to Mr. Latham; "Tomorrow is Another Day". Then she thought of the following; "Another Day"; "Tote the Heavy Load"; "Milestones"; "Bah. Bah. Black Sheep"; "Not So Blind"; "Not In Our Stars"; and "Bugle Song".

One day, tired of trying to think of more titles, she decided to read some poetry, which she always enjoyed. She picked up a book at random and flipping through it her eyes fell on a poem entitled "Cynara" by Ernest Dawson, one of her favorite poets.

At the front of each stanza was this: "I have been faithful to thee, Cynara in my fashion; I forgot much Cynara, Gone With the Wind!"

"That's it," Miss Mitchell screamed. Then her faithful maid, Bessie Jordan rushed in the room, asking in an exciting voice, "Are you alright Miss Margaret?" She answered, "This is it!"

After that she sent a wire to Mr. Latham, giving him the title. So, that is how *Gone With the Wind* was born. As many have heard, Miss Mitchell wrote the last chapter of her epic novel first.

The following letter from Margaret Mitchell of November 9, 1936 reveals the source of the title to GONE WITH THE WIND.

I took the title of my book from the third verse of a poem by Ernest Dawson, commonly called "Cynara." The full title of the poem is "Non Sum Qualis Eram Bonae Sub Regno Cynarae". However, the title of my book has no connection with the thoughts expressed in Dawson's poem. It happened to be the phrase I wanted so I lifted it from the poem.

Cordially,

Margaret Mitchell Marsh.

Photo Section

Pre-Book
Era

Margaret at the age of 14.

Teenage Margaret.

Margaret at the age of 18.

Margaret in 1920.

Margaret starring in her own production of Thomas Dixon's, *The Traitor*.

Budding authoress. School annual published one of her stories in her senior
year.

Sophie Henker and Margaret ready for riding.

Cutting up with lifelong friend Augusta Dearborn.

Margaret and A.S. Weil doing "The Apache Dance" at a Charity Ball.

Star reporter for *Atlanta Journal Sunday Magazine.*

Interviewing Rudolph Valentino.

Interviewing Georgia Tech students.

Posing for an illustration for one of her articles.

John Marsh's favorite picture of Margaret.

John Marsh.

Marrying the wrong man, said her brother Stephens (far right).

YOLANDE GWIN

I received the following letters from Margaret Mitchell in 1936.

Monday, February 10, 1936

Atlanta, Ga.

Dear Yolande,
     Until I read your article about me, I didn't really feel like an author. I've worked so hard and been so tired and sick that the only emotion I could feel was one of numbed relief that the stuff was out of my hands and in the mail. And I wasn't thrilled or excited, as I've always heard authors are. And I felt irritably, that I was being cheated out of whatever fun there was in writing.
     But when I saw that you had given me the headline and written at such length and said so many marvelous things, my heart began to bump and I stopped feeling numb and suddenly, I felt like an author! And I thank you not only for your kind words but for bringing me back to life again. But, Yolande, you are going to answer to the Recording Angel for all the nice fibs you told about me!
     I wish I was as smart and clever as you said I was but I do thank you for saying I was.

Later —

I ran into Mrs. J.M. Couper and she told me that you had a grand job on a Washington paper and was leaving town immediately. Why didn't you say something about it when we were talking over the phone? I've tried to get you by phone but your line keeps busy so I'm writing you my congratulations. Working in Washington would be an adventure. I've always heard that only the cream of the newspaper profession get jobs there so I'm proud to know you.
     Jacques Furtrell's, who worked on the Journal with me years ago is on the "Star" I think. If you run into him, give him my love. And Coleman Jones on the N.Y Herald Tribune Bureau is a good friend too. I hope you have the best luck in the world and are very happy there.

Peggy Mitchell

Atlanta, Ga.

June 28, 1936

Dear Yolande;

I wish there were ten or a dozen ways of saying "What a swell story!" But unless I run amok and use such movie words a "Stupendous!" "Magnificent!" "Colossal!" I think of no better phrasing than, with a simple dignity, to say "What a swell story!"

I never dreamed you were going to give me so much space. I thought, as the resume of the story was so long, that you'd just give an introductory paragraph and let me ride. And I'd have ridden, just as happy as a nigger at a hog killing. But all that space, so long a story, so completely flattering a story — well, I'm still blushing about the ankles, as Jurgen once remarked.

And oh, Yolande, how nice of you to refer to me as a "young author!" Me, who have passed the broiling stage and the frying stage and am rapidly approaching the roasting and baking stage. And what a good lead. I've read a lot of stories on this book and on me and none of them had as different and clever a lead. That "Marching through Georgia" idea was a honey. I am mailing it to Mr. Latham today and I know he will be tickled and pleased, as tickled and pleased as I am. I can't get over all the nice things you said, not only about the book but about me and my style and my "poisonality". For such perjury you will have to answer on Judgement Day but I hope I will be there to put in a good word for you with Recording Angel and explain that you had such a kind heart you could never resist white lies about friends.

But what a time I shall have trying to live up to all the things you said. How can I appear as erudite as you made me out to be?

When this cruel war is over and I am published and I get time to breathe, I intend to call by the office and buy you a dope (yes, I don't care how I spend my money) and tell you at the top of my voice how much I appreciate it all.

With love and thanks,

Peggy

P.S. And I was pretty happy to see the big by-line you got, too.

The following information was given to me by Marianna Goldsmith of Atlanta, Georgia. She married John Knox of Atlanta. After his death, she married Leonard P. Eager 228 West Main St. Evansville, Wis.

MARIANNA KNOX

The following is the letter the former Marianna Goldsmith wrote me when I enquired if she remembered Margaret Mitchell. She wrote:

"Yes, of course I knew her but Margaret was older than I. She was in John Knox's class at Tenth Street School. He often laughed about how he dipped her pigtails in his inkwell and how furious she was. Her friend also in the class was Edgarta Horton. John said they wrote stories and plays all the time. While others were playing and socializing, they were writing exotic tales continuously.

When I was in high school, and lived most of the year at East Lake, I spent half the time with my aunt, Mrs. W.H. (Annie Fitten) Glenn. She lived on Peachtree Street between 16th and 17th streets and it was a convenient place to have dates pick me up. The McCulloughs lived on one side, Dr. and Mrs. Bates Block on the other side and Lelia Kirkpatrick across the street. Peggy Mitchell lived a block down across the street. Peggy found out that my uncle, Billy Glenn bought a book or two a week — everything from *Who Done Its* to historical novels. He had many filled book cases and my aunt told Peggy that she was welcome to borrow books. At least once a week, Peggy would appear with a stack of books to return, as many as she could carry. She would put them back carefully and select another load. We were all amazed how she could read so much so quickly!"

"Peggy Mitchell was someone I always knew. Atlanta was not big and we both grew up there. Her father, Eugene Mitchell, was a great friend of my grandfather, Jere W. Goldsmith, who lived in the Goldsmith apartments at Peachtree and 11th street. Mr. Mitchell came to see "Pa" often and they would discuss their favorite subject, the War Between The States. I'm sure Mr. Mitchell dicsussed the subject at home with Peggy and Stephens, her brother, very often.

When I was Iris Lee at Davison's (in the 30s) it was a unique job, a combination of people relations and personal shopping.

One day Raymond Kline, President of Davison's called me to his office. He wanted to ask my advice as P.R. Director, Macmillan Publishers were coming out with a book by an Atlanta woman and Davison's had been offered the pre-publication autographing party. He wanted to know if we — the store, should go all out for the occasion or just have a small affair. I asked, "Who is the author?" "She is Margaret Mitchell and the book is about the Civil War and Atlanta."

"Oh, Peggy Mitchell" I said. "I have known her always and I don't believe she could write anything earth shattering." (Sometimes you are too close and can't see the forest for the trees.) "I think we should have a *little* party in the book department, run a small ad and let her autograph her book for those who come in." I also added that we should reduce the book $.25. The publication price was to be $3.00. I advised that we sell it that day for $2.75, which we did!

My advice to Raymond Kline was probably the worse public relations advice ever given. Ripley should have quoted it in his "Believe It Or Not" column. I knew "Home Town Peggy" well and we think a genius is always miles away.

To swell the crowd in the book department on party day. I asked my mother, Mrs. Paul Goldsmith, to be sure and be there. Mama had a small income and received her check the first of each month. She always bought presents galore for everyone when the check arrived. We told her she spent money like a drunken sailor on pay day. Mama came to the pre-publication party, bought the book and inscribed it. "To Marianna, from the drunken sailor, July 2, 1936!" Margaret Mitchell dutifully autographed it. A little later Peggy wouldn't autograph a copy for anyone, even her bosses at the *Atlanta Journal.*

The minute I began reading "Gone With the Wind" I was hooked and couldn't put it down — like everyone else. When I wasn't at work, I spent as much time as possible at the Piedmont Driving Club swimming pool. With me went GONE WITH THE WIND so it unavoidably got wet and beat up. Today, all the worse for wear, I prize my autographed First Edition as much as anything I own!

In 1943, Charles Jagels succeeded Raymond Kline as the president of Davison's and the two of us founded Atlanta's "Woman of the Year Organization." Women were honored in various fields of endeavor and on the evening of the big banquet one was named Atlanta's Woman of the Year for that particular year. Everyone on the Board or a Committee the first year agreed that no one *had* or *could* ever eclipse Margaret Mitchell. But Margaret Mitchell had published her book in 1936 and this was supposed to be an accomplishment of 1943. So it was decided to present Margaret Mitchell with a huge bouquet of American Beauty Roses and name her "Atlanta's Woman of *All* Years."

She was elected to the Board of Trustees of W.O.T.Y. at the next meeting and she served on it with enthusiasm for many years. I was in charge of arranging all the W.O.T.Y. luncheon meetings at the Capital City Club and she asked me to see that an empty Coca Cola crate was put at her place under the table so she could always rest her feet on it. She was tiny and short and needed a footrest.

Peggy Mitchell was a great humanitarian with a warm heart. She was very keen on discovering some unknown little "woman" who was doing an outstanding job in the community with no recognition. There was a woman who worked at the city jail looking after women prisoners. Peggy had become her friend through newspaper work. Peggy wrote letter after letter to the committee men who made the selection for W.O.T.Y. awards. She wanted so much for her to be honored. But her candidate was never selected because she was paid for her job and a volunteer was selected.

Bill (W.D.) Ellis and the late R.L. (Trot) Foreman shared the same birthdays. On their 50th birthday, their wives gave them a surprise party. By telegrams all guests were ordered to wear costumes — something related to old days in Atlanta. We all met at the Piedmont Driving Club before being taken by bus to the old Kimball House downtown. I decided to be Belle Watling of *Gone With The Wind*. My costume was daring with black net stockings and a light bustle. Margaret Mitchell and husband, John Marsh happened to be at the Driving Club that night for dinner and Peggy got a big laugh over my rendition of Belle. She was always ready to see the fun in everything. Incidentally I won the prize for the best costume — a bottle of champagne.

ALLISON

Mrs. Robert W. Allison, the former "Bitsy" Sims, has many memories of her friendship with Margaret Mitchell. In addition, she has her memorabilia inherited from her late mother, Mrs. Luise [sic] Sims. One is now a priceless and sentimental item — an autographed first edition of *Gone With The Wind.*

Mrs. Allison also related how her mother was always interested, as well as being a participant, in literary and book clubs in Atlanta.

The late Raymond Kline was president of Davison-Paxon Store (now Macy's) in Atlanta during the thirties. One time during that period, he asked Mrs. Sims if she could help out in the store's book department during the holidays (Christmas and New Years). Her answer was "Yes, but I would want the days off to attend the meetings of my literary clubs." Her request was granted.

When Mrs. Allison received the publishers' (Macmillan) rough draft of *Gone With The Wind,* she placed an order for several editions of the book with an inner feeling that the book would sell. She informed Mr. Kline that she had a best seller for the store in *Gone With The Wind.* Adding that, "I know it will win the Pulitzer Prize." Mr. Kline bet her $50.00 that it wouldn't.

An afternoon tea was given in the store's tea room honoring Margaret Mitchell on publication day in June 1936.

Mrs. Allison, at that time was Bitsy Sims and was in the junior class at the North Avenue Presbyterian School. (It was a private school in Atlanta and located on Ponce de Leon Avenue.) It was later merged with another private school, Washington Seminary located on Peachtree Road just south of Brookwood Rail Station. The two schools became the Westminister School, which is also a private school.

She and a classmate, Dot Davis, who later married Harry Gwinner, served punch to a very small and limited number of guests.

Later, the book swept the nation and that year, 1936, it won the Pulitzer Prize and at the time Mr. Kline and his wife were on a world tour and heard the exciting news. Mr. Kline called Mrs. Sims — "I've just heard the news about the Mitchell book. Your $50.00 check is on the way!"

"In May, 1941, Mother gave me a trousseau tea," said Mrs. Allsion. They were quite the thing in those days. Peggy Mitchell came to the party and in her cute daring ways showed us a bit of her lingerie — white cotton, knee-length bloomers! Mrs. Allison continued by saying, "Peggy had a mind of devotion to the Confederacy."

She and mother went together to Oakland Cemetery on Confederate Memorial Day to place the flags and flowers on the graves of the Confederate dead.

On July 2, 1936, Margaret Mitchell wrote the following letter to Mrs. Sims;

> *Gone With The Wind* and I owe a lot to you. You believed in the success of the book long before I did. What's more, you backed up your faith by taking the risk that it would sell. Anyone who reads the book knows how much I appreciate and admire people who have the courage to take risks when their judgement tells them it is the right thing to do. You are that sort and you have helped a lot to make the book a success in Atlanta, which means more to me than if it sells a million, elsewhere.
>
> Yours, Margaret Mitchell.

It is now a cherished letter of Mrs. Allison. As of 1986, Gone With The Wind *has sold over 25 million copies.*

Margaret wrote many letters to friends.

HAMILTON

When Mrs. Alice Hamilton's book, Blue Ridge Mountains Memories, *was published, she was quite thrilled and happy.*

Her daughter Sarah (Mrs. Sarah Edwards) had been urging and urging her to write. Mrs. Hamilton, a native of Jefferson County, Georgia, was living in Atlanta when her book was published. In a recent interview she said:

"We, that is my late husband, Capt. Hamilton (a sea captain) and I, moved here in 1928. We ran the Northwood Hotel. It was on 17th Street and there were 40 rooms and baths. We did not serve meals, so everybody would go to a tea room up on Peachtree Street. The people who lived at our hotel were actually permanent residents. After my husband died, I continued to run the hotel for about 10 years. My sister, Ruth McGuire of Knoxville, Tenn., lived there with me for about nine years.

Next to the hotel which Mrs. Hamilton and her second husband ran was an apartment in which lived "a very attractive couple named Mr. and Mrs. Marsh."

She used to come over a lot to swap stories with my husband about his experiences as a sea captain. He was not well during his last years, and she would pop in and bring baskets of fruit and some nice dinner dishes. We were soon calling her Margaret and we just loved her.

"We never knew that she was writing a book until the news broke that she had sold it and called it *Gone With the Wind.* Naturally, we, as well as the other guests at the hotel, which we then owned, were just thrilled to death. Of course, when the book became such a sensation, she was besieged with company, reporters and all sorts of curious-minded people banging at her door. She just could not cope with it. So, one night she came over and asked if she could have ONE room to hide in and try to catch up with her mail. She and her secretary, Margaret Baugh, would come over early in the morning and stay all day. No one ever knew that she had a hide-away right next door to her own apartment. None of the other guests ever mentioned it for they wanted to comply with her wishes. When the time came for her to stop auto-graphing books and writing letters to unknowns with her personal sig-natures, she went back to her own apartment. She just spent the day at my place as her husband (John Marsh) was at their apartment. She paid the rent with a check, signed of course. It was for $32.50 for the month's rent. I wanted to save it because it had her signature, but before it was deposited, my late son had a copy made of it. She was a great person and I loved her. Fame did not go to her head.

The apartment at 17th Street.

MRS. W.O. MOODY

Mrs. W.O. Moody, now living in Greenville, Ohio on Tannery Hill, as the former Minnie Hite, worked on the Journal Magazine *staff for many years and knew Margaret Mitchell — she wrote the following letter:*

Tannery Hill, 635 Newark Road, Granville, Ohio 43023
January 17, 1982

Dear Yolande:

Now to your request, and let me just ramble along and see what turns up that you can sort out and use if you wish, You have a great title, *I Knew Peggy Mitchell*, but are handicapped by the fact that many of those who did know her best are beyond communication. The Perkersons, and Eleanor and O.B. Keeler, for instance. Actually, though we were close friends for years, and had the additional bond of sharing The Macmillan Company as our publishers, and the friendship of Harold Latham, Vice President, then in charge of trade. I wonder sometimes whether or not I ever *really* knew Peggy, or who, if anyone, really knew her. After her death, and in his later years, Harold tried to induce me by every means possible to write a brief book about her — the sort of memoir Vincent Sheen wrote of Edna St. Vincent Millay (*The Indigo Bunting*, Schocken Books, 1973) and I always refused saying, "Harold, I honestly feel that I didn't know her well enough." But I was into other projects by then, and we moved up here when Coach retired in Atlanta, and Harold died, and I was into a different book for Macmillan.

I hesitate to say just when or under what circumstances I first met Peggy. I seem to remember a small cocktail party at Ellen Wolff's on Peachtree Place. I do very well recall the first time my husband and I attended a party of Peggy's when she and John lived on 17th Street and *Gone With The Wind* was in the process of publication. The *only* time we appeared together as young authors was when *Gone With The Wind* and my second novel *Death Is a Little Man* were about to come out and Mrs. Emma Garret Morris was in her heyday of giving "literary talks." Peggy and I were nearly scared out of our wits, but we did our duty. I believe that was the only time Peggy got up on her feet and talked about her book, and I did as little of it as possible. I don't recall how Mrs. Morris got us to appear on that occasion, but she was a dear person and we both liked and admired her.

One good friend of Peggy's you may not remember, is Edith Howe Davis (Mrs. Legare Davis) who in the days of the hectic publicity over Gone With The Wind lived at Hootin' Owl Farm a few miles outside Atlanta, and often in that first summer, Peggy would escape there for respite. It was a place almost impossible to find, so she felt safe there.

Yes, I remember how pleased Peggy was with the interview you wrote of her when, or just before, her book came out, and one of her most hilarious stories (which I heard her tell several times) was about your great chase of Honey Chile Timmons at the Terminal Station, as Honey Chile was in turn trying to chase down Mr. Cukor. Of course I read your account of it at the time. Good writing.

Peggy was always awfully good to my children. One time she happened upon my older daughter, Elizabeth, on one of the upper floors at Rich's, and somehow got hold of two bottles of Coca-Cola and she and Elizabeth sat down to enjoy them. This was at the very peak of publicity, when everyone was fighting to get a close look at Margaret Mitchell or perhaps have a word with her. As she and Elizabeth were peacefully sitting there, sipping and chatting, the elevator doors opened and out came some eager-beaver type women, who immediately spied them. To Peggy's horror they hastened her way, but as if she didn't notice, she stood up and whisked Elizabeth and the Cokes through the doors into the mysterious depths of the working parts of that floor, and they finished their visit sitting on mattresses safely beyond a sign reading Employees only — No Admittance.

Which story takes me to Davison's, and the Atlanta visit of the then popular British author who wrote The Miniver, but I can't think of her name. Anyhow, this young woman, who must have been about the age of Peggy and me (her husband was at the time fighting the war (World War II) in North Africa, and she was on an autographing tour in this country, and I believe to visit her children who had been sent out of England for saftey during the air raids, were making a tour of the store after one of those luncheons honoring a visiting author, and for no reason I can explain at the moment, found ourselves on the furniture floor with before us a vast expanse of beds and mattresses. No customers in sight — just a few dignified salesmen, hands clasped behind them eyeing us warily and no doubt recognizing Peggy and me, but giving no sign, just waiting to see what we were up to.

The visiting author, having come through the blitz, and with her husband at the front, was certainly under great stress, and so were Peggy and I, it being wartime, my fifth novel *Long Meadows* about to be published, or perhaps later published, Peggy, under the strain of the vast success of *Gone With The Wind*. I still don't know what possessed us, but with one accord we took off to jump on the inviting mattresses on display, leaping from one to another with complete disregard for the properties. When at last we came down to earth, straightening our hats and clothing (yes, we wore hats in those days) the girl from England said, "Oh, I feel so much better!" Peggy replied, "A good romp was just what we needed." The salesmen throughout had remained in full dignity, but they gazed on us fondly.

As the war progressed, my younger daughter, Mary Lou, had graduated from college, and was working as a microscopist at he Georgia State Board of Health. Not yet formally engaged to a fine young man somewhere flying the skies in a bomber, she became increasingly involved with young Dr. Bartolome Prieto, whose country, Paraguay, had sent him to Atlanta to learn about Georgia's public health program, as his country and Georgia at that time had about the same problems. He was assigned to work with Mary Lou at her microscope; almost every evening he accompanied her home to dinner, and as his country was not at war he made a pleasant escort to the Ansley Roof where he and Mary Lou enjoyed hours of dancing the samba. He was in Atlanta a year, and was to return to his own country, the young couple decided that they would marry. Mary Lou could not go home with him, as she could obtain neither transportation nor visa.

Our friends were up in arms. "You can't let that beautiful child marry a stranger about whom you know nothing," they chorused. "He may never come back. What do you know of his people? What about their religious differences?"

Gasoline rationing was on, and we lived quite a distance from town. But here came Peggy. She said, "If Tolo has sat at your table for meals, and behaved like a gentleman, you know how he has been brought up, and the kind of family he comes from. If he and Mary Lou are in love, don't stand in their way."

Their marriage lasted until his death — 35 happy years, with Tolo rapidly rising in the corporate hierarchy of one of the world's foremost pharmaceutical companies.

I try to think of actual remarks Peggy made — what she said on various occasions. One time we were downtown in the late afternoon when she suddenly recalled that she had left no orders for the evening meal, and, worse, her household was at a low ebb of supplies. It was when they lived in the little apartment on 17th Street, near Peachtree. She worried a moment; then said, "Oh, well, Bessie (meaning her cook, Bessie Jordan) will know what to do. Why, Bessie can even get credit at Kroger's, which is more than I can."

As for all those who so intimately claimed to know Margaret Mitchell, Peggy held herself all the more aloof. I especially recall women who had been her classmates at Washington Seminary, but in no sense close friends. Some of them even wrote articles stressing their friendship and tried to get them published in *The Atlanta Journal* or it's Sunday Magazine. Editor John Paschall in his gentle way deplored this situation. "Angus, what shall I do?" I once heard him say to Angus Perkerson, in genuine distress. "This writer is a prominent woman. She would regard a rejection as insult."

"Too bad," replied Angus. "If we let everyone on who wants to get on the bandwagon, the thing will break down."

Peggy was a great storyteller, and one of her best (which I'm sure you have heard many times) was about the first breakfast she experienced as a freshman at Smith College. A dubious-appearing substance had been deposited on her bread-and-butter plate, but as she never in her life had eaten breakfast without a hot biscuit, she waited for them.

However, a sturdy northern-type girl reached over and said, "If you don't want your toast, do you care if I have it?" Peggy complied politely, but as she always ended the story, "So that was toast? I had heard about, but I never had seen it. And there it was, nothing in the world but scorched light bread."

If you have almost completed your book, you may not have read whatever bit you may sift out of this rambling letter. The Journal "family," as John Paschall used to describe it, was closely knit during the years I was writing the column for it — the Perkersons, Peggy and John Marsh, the Keelers, Frank Daniel, Miss Emily Woodward of Vienna, Ga., whenever she was in town, the Jimmy Popes and then the Wright Bryans; Coach and myself. With a few others coming and going. You know who they were. Those of us with no children, or whose children were grown, always got together on Christmas Eve at the Keeler's *Distillery Hill.*

One of life's mysteries Peggy and I never were able to figure out was why our cooks, Bessie Jordan and Donnie Douglas, always kept a glass of water with a slice of lemon in it in our respective refrigerators. When we questioned, the answer we always got was, "Oh, dat! What you askin' any question 'bout dat for?" So we never knew.

Yes, everything is going along well with me, or as well as can be, since Coach passed away six years ago. We came up here when he retired in Atlanta, as I inherited my Yankee grandfather's homeplace, house built 1806. I immediately went to work on the book-reviewing staff of *The Columbus Dispatch,* and kept an earlier promise to write a daily column for The Newark, Ohio, *Advocate,* Democratic since 1820 except for three years during the 1860s when Lincoln had it suspended because it had come out so strongly for John C. Breckenridge in the 1860 campaign. The column ran for 17 years, along with a morning and evening radio (WCLT) program, but I recently gave it up, as the newspaper has changed beyond recognition after being sold to Lord Thompson of London, who owns about 15 other Ohio newspapers. I still review for *The Dispatch,* and am trying to finish the novel long under contract.

My best wishes to you and your book.

Sincerely,

Minnie Moody

MRS. GORDON CATTS

Mrs. Gordon Catts, the former Frances Austin, is a graduate of Atlanta's fashionable girls private school, Washington Seminary.
She recalls one "fun" incident.

"Each year," she says "Miss Emma (Emma Scott, principal of the Seminary) would entertain at an afternoon tea for the graduates who later became members of the Atlanta Debutante Club. I was a member of the 1935-36 Atlanta Debutante Club.

"She had the tea in the long wide entrance hall of the large white columned home on Peachtree which became the home of the boarding students from throughout the School.

"Miss Emma and all of us stood in the receiving line to greet the visitors. We all wore long formal afternoon attire and stood in line receiving for one and a half hours greeting guests.

"About the end of the party, all of us took off our high-heeled slippers and stood in our stocking feet to greet the late-comers. To our horror in came Margaret Mitchell! A former graduate, speaking and chatting with all the debutantes.

"As she came closer to us — three or four chums, we tried to gain her attention by grabbing and holding her hands as we talked so we wouldn't look down and see us minus shoes.. Finally she left and waved goodbye to us and saying, "I've stood in line a long time too! I know!"

ADAIR

Margaret Mitchell was a graduate of Washington Seminary and granted an interview to Mary Virginia McConnell (now Mrs. A.D. Adair Jr.) to appear in the Missemma Magazine *published by the seminary and filled with stories of and by students. The interview follows:*

Margaret Mitchell was curled up in a large armchair Friday morning–appeared to this reporter more like a school girl than a famous author. Her dress, with puffed sleeves was trimmed with large orange buttons matching the walls and draperies around her. "People expect me to be dressed in hooped skirts and lace petticoats because they associate me with the setting of the book" she told Miss McConnell. Having written her book wearing slacks and shirts, she was completely out of clothes when the book was published, and also being at home and receiving so many people, she was forced to buy some dresses.

Miss Mitchell's first attempt to shop was completely futile, she recalled as a group of ladies invaded her dressing room and made such remarks as "isn't she skinny?" and "she's awfully short."   And not desiring to be an object of observation, she left. The next attempt for dress buying was accompanied by a lady who gasped at the fact that Miss Mitchell did not have lace on her petticoat and added, "If I had made five million dollars like you, I'd have my petticoats trimmed in lace!" Miss Mitchell protested that she had not made five million dollars and furthermore, she said she didn't have lace on petticoats. "I have never seen her before," said Miss Mitchell, "and finally I left in despair."

MANRY

Mrs. William Manry III, the former Georgia Hoyle Adams made her debut as a member of the 1939 Atlanta Debutante Club.

They, the debutantes were avid admirers of Margaret Mitchell and her book, so they labeled themselves, "Gone With the Wind" debutantes on their debut year of 1939. That same year was the world premiere of the *Gone With The Wind* movie here in Atlanta.

The former Miss Adams attended Washington Seminary the exclusive private school in Atlanta located just south of the Brookwood Rail Station and also amid a plush neighborhood of prominent Atlantans. The Seminary was later merged with the North Avenue Presbyterian School, also a private institution, to form the present Westminister Schools.

Miss Adams was editor-in-chief of the Seminary annual titled *"Facts and Fancies"* during her senior year, 1939. The annual that year was dedicated to Margaret Mitchell who graduated from the Seminary in 1918. Miss Mitchell served as literary editor of the annual the year she graduated.

The foreword in the 1939 annual was written by Georgia Adams who also wrote the dedication. She was also elected "Spirit of the Seminary."

Miss Adams was on the Senior Round Table, one of the highest honors at the school, and was also in the annual May Day court. Also in the annual was the class song, the Alma Mater. Frances Austin, now Mrs. Gordon Catts wrote the music and the late Claire Haverty who later became Mrs. Frank Ridley Jr. wrote the words. Mary Fort Ligon a member of the faculty, served as the senior class sponsor.

Sue Clapp was class president; Elizabeth Colley was vice-president; Florence Jones, secretary and Margaret L'Engle was treasurer.

WILLET

The late Mrs. Lawrence Willet was the former Julia Brantley of Blackshear, Ga. After her marriage, she and her husband lived in Atlanta. She was a member of the Atlanta Junior League and wrote the following for the Junior League Magazine:

MARGARET MITCHELL

by Julia B. Willet

"I made every bit of it up in my own head, and you ask the next person who tells you he knows where Tara is to show me — I'd like to see it," said Margaret Mitchell, sitting with her feet doubled up under her, in a big armchair in her pretty apartment.

This was in response to a question of burning interest in local circles where everyone has a different idea as to the location of Tara, which has been claimed to be the ancestral home of many. There has also been much speculation as to the identity of Scarlett, Rhett, and Melanie.

"The characters were all purely imaginary," Miss Mitchell said. "But I've had people tell me that I described their Grandpa Butler perfectly, but they did not think I should have used his real name! Others have said that of course they knew it was their Grandpa and how nice of me not to use the family name! And although there never was in Atlanta such a house as the one Scarlett built in the book, one lady told me that her mother went to the ball Scarlett gave there! In spite of all this I still say I made it all up!"

In fact, so careful was she to avoid any actual situations that she got a copy of Sherman's war map of 1864 which had all the houses in the vicinity of Tara plotted on it, and picked out a ten-mile stretch which had no settlements, to locate the plantations of the story. She followed the same method with old Atlanta maps to locate Aunt Pittypat's, Scarlett's, and the other houses.

Miss Mitchell says she started the book so long ago she can't remember how she happened to do it, except that she thinks a sprained ankle and the resulting sheer boredom brought it on, added to the fact that "so many dull books were published that winter, there didn't seem to be anything for me to do but write one myself!"

She says, "I never used a notebook in my life. If I had to look up everything I wouldn't enjoy writing." She planned *Gone with the Wind* to the last word of conversation before she ever sat down to the typewriter.

"I knew these people as well as you know your friends," she went on. "So there could never be any doubt as to what they would do or say in a given situation. I didn't write the chapters in sequence — in fact, I wrote the last one first, and sold the book without the first chapter being completed! Suppose I got bored with chapter five — I wanted to write about love, and here I was stuck with the Battle of Atlanta. Why sit glaring at that paragraph when I could go on to chapter sixty and write about love! Very often your subconscious will work out the problem you've been stuck on, and then you can come back and grab that paragraph when it least suspects it! The only time I ever made notes was if I had an idea in the night and didn't want to get out of bed to write it.'

In answer to the question if she had regular hours for work, Miss Mitchell said, "I had regular hours for work but I never kept them. Every time I started to write, some one of my family or friends would have a baby or a neurosis, or get desperately ill, and that would keep me so busy, being the only girl in the family, that sometimes I couldn't write more than ten minutes a day, although once in a while I could write a chapter at a sitting. I heartily advocate regular hours for young writers — even if I don't keep them myself." . . .

Every chapter in the first draft of *Gone With The Wind* was re-written at least twenty times.

"I rewrote the first chapter seventy times," Miss Mitchell said, looking extremely youthful in her dainty brown and white dress, with her short curly auburn hair. (She says she and Mary Pickford were the last two women in the world to bob.) "For six years whenever I didn't have anything else to do, I rewrote the first chapter. It became a kind of game to see how many ways I could write it. When the book was sold it didn't have a first chapter because I was rewriting it at the time. And when it actually went to press with the seventieth draft, I wrote another, and telegraphed my publishers that I had revised it again. They telegraphed back that that would doubtless continue to be so, but the book had gone to press then, and nothing more could be changed!"

Miss Mitchell never studied short-story writing or journalism, but was on the staff of the *Atlanta Journal* for four years and loved the varied experience it gave her.

"I don't know about technique," she said. "I was asked to give a talk to some college girls on that subject, and had to admit I didn't know what it was."

She went on, "I was terrified when I heard the publishers had ordered ten thousand copies of my book to be printed. Five thousand was the maximum amount I had expected, but they assured me they could work off the extra copies on the Christmas trade." The book has sold over 500,000 copies!

"It was a book that any of us brought up here in the South could have written," she insisted, "just from listening to Grandpa or old Aunt Janey talk. The time always seemed more real to me than my own. I just opened up my memory and it all came out. I never referred to a history or a reference book until my book was sold, and then I checked and verified every fact. There were just a few places where I left blanks to be filled in later, where I wasn't absolutely sure of a distance or a date, but the rest was all right there in my head."

Old scrapbooks, letters and diaries are the best sources for background in a historical novel, Miss Mitchell says, and added that she "bumped over country roads a mountain goat would have had trouble in navigating" in her search for accurate description.

She pointed to the huge stack of mail that had just come in. "Three quarters of those letters will ask the same question," she said, " 'Did Scarlett win Rhett back?' I have to answer truthfully that I don't know. I never thought of it as being a tricky ending. To me it seemed the logical one considering their two characters. Their destinies seemed written on their foreheads, and to me it was the natural place to end. I can't imagine what happened next. And no one will ever know for I shan't write a sequel.

"In fact I hope I'll never write another book at all. I'd rather scrub floors, pick cotton, or take an automobile to pieces than write another. There's material enough in the exciting and interesting field of the War and Reconstruction to write a million more, but I don't want to do it. That awful feeling of waking up every morning and knowing the book isn't finished, and you hope an earthquake or an avalanche will come so you don't have to work that day! I hate the mental and physical work of it!"

"I never thought of selling my book," Miss Mitchell went on. "I didn't think anybody would be interested in reading about the War between the States, unless maybe a few schools or colleges could use it for a reference book, but I've had letters from California and from people in logging camps in Canada, all expressing interest in this part of our country and our history."

When Mr. Latham of the Macmillan Company came south looking for a novel, Miss Mitchell was invited to lunch with him.

"Everyone else was busy that afternoon," she said, "so I took him for a ride to see the dogwood in bloom. By the time we got back, he inveigled me into letting him have my manuscript, and if his train hadn't left twenty minutes later, I'd have snatched it back! He got the worst of it, though," she added with a laugh, "for he thought it would be a tiny little thing, and there it was in sixty manila envelopes, for I didn't have time to strip all the alternate chapters I'd written. There weren't but three chapters in the book that didn't have several versions.

"And that's all," she said. "And I don't think I've said much that could be very helpful to any other writer. I just had to do it the way it comes natural to me."

Editor's Note: Margaret Mitchell sent the following to Mrs. Willet regarding the above article.

The interview is so very good, so accurate, that I feel pickayunish indeed in lighting upon small minor matters. I hope you'll understand when I ask you to omit mention of the cigarette in paragraph one. This is why. My father doesn't know I smoke. Yes, I know that sounds foolish and Victorian but it's true! I wouldn't want him to be hurt about it.

On page two, in paragraph one, there is some confusion due to the fact that on the previous page you have spoken of Scarlett's house in Atlanta and this first paragraph of page two refers to houses in the County. If you inserted after "in the vicinity'" the words "of Tara" or of "Clayton County" or some phrase to identify the locality and show that you have moved from town to country. Or else switch the second sentence forward and make it the first sentence of the paragraph.

I know this sounds foolish but in paragraph three, page two you use the word "pen". Of course, it's used figuratively. But a lot of your readers may wonder. You see, so many letters I receive from young and new writers ask the question, "Do you compose on the typewriter or in pencil or pen?" I do not know why this matter should be of importance to writers but it seems to be so. I am tongue-tied with a pen or a pencil and can only compose on a typewriter.

My husband says he doesn't want to be a "very nice man". I do not know why this should be for the fact remains that he is indeed a very nice man, no matter what he says to the contrary. But could you just say. . . ." Made my debut and married."?

In the matter of my mathematics, my husband, instead of Bessie, the cook, balances my bank book. The invaluable Bessie handles the fractions that inevitably arise on the shopping list at the A and P. and the Piggly Wiggly. (page 4, paragraph2)

Page 4, paragraph 2, I know that I used the word "malingering" but on thinking it over and looking it up I realize that I used it wrongly. Malingering applies generally to a person who evades duties through a pretense of illness. I was as strong as a Percheron at the time — so I guess I misled you on that word. Could you make it "I passed with such perfect marks. . . . but I forgot it all the next day"?

Page six, paragraph two — I know I said "I could write a million more" and you were quite right in so quoting me. But I didn't make my meaning clear. I meant that there is material for a million books in the War and Reconstruction period. I never saw so rich a field, or so interesting a field or so exciting and tantalizing a field for research and for writing. But I couldn't write another book! . . . I realize, as I hear my words read back to me from your article that I sound as though I thought airily that I could turn out another *Gone With The Wind* with a mere twist of the wrist and, alas, such is not so. Writing is so dreadfully hard for me, such a tedious task and I do it so slowly.

I know that you will think from the foregoing page that I didn't like the interview and that I pulled it all to pieces. But that isn't so. I thought — and so did John who is an ex-newspaper man — that it was a grand job. I do not know if you know it but it is rare indeed to find some one (who hasn't had years of newspaper experience) who can follow a person who is talking fast and leaping from one subject to the other — and make the interview coherent. It is rarer still to find a writer who can pick up the idiom of the person interviewed and put it upon paper so that the words sound natural. That takes an "ear" like an ear for music.

Thank you so very much for the interview. I'll look forward to seeing the print.

Sincerely

Margaret Mitchell

P.S. I have to go to the eye doctor's so early this morning and as the cook is going to be off today I thought I'd send this on to you, knowing you wanted it quickly.

VAN KULLER

Mrs. Matthew Van Kuller, former Eugenia Snow said she took lessons from Mrs. Eva Lovett. Several recitals on stage at a local auditorium were given during the years.

Mrs. Van Kuller recalls one recital she was in where all the dancers had to change costumes several times during the performance.

There was such a nice little lady in the dressing room who would look after us and help us get into a different outfit. She would call all of us "Honey" and was so much fun all the time. We called her Mrs. Marsh as Miss Lovett told us to do.

When *Gone With The Wind* came out only then did I realize that the nice little lady was Margaret Mitchell.

THOMAS

Mrs. W. Wailes Thomas, the former Elizabeth Scott thought her friend Peggy Mitchell had always been a great storyteller and would enliven groups she was with — always full of fun.

I remember giving a tea at my home. Peggy was invited and came.

I introduced her to some of the guests as "Mrs. Marsh," as I didn't want my guests to intrude upon her while at the party. It would have ruined the day for Peggy as I knew how she was.

Several days after the tea party, some of the guests called me and raised cain because I did not say Mrs. Marsh was Peggy Mitchell.

THE GEORGIA OF GONE WITH THE WIND

BY YOLANDE GWIN

The following is reprinted from the June 1937 Behind the Wheel, Southern Travel Magazine *Atlanta Motor Club.*

A young woman who has made literary history has inadvertently brought thousands of visitors to Georgia.

She is Margaret Mitchell, author of the world-famous and now Pultizer Prize winning novel, *Gone With The Wind.*

They come from north, east, south and west. They come by plane, by train, but more often by motor, in an effort to fully cover and to see the historic spots which have made the nation Georgia-conscious since Miss Mitchell's book was published.

Their questions and their requests are always the same. They want to go to Jonesboro. They want to see Tara, Twleve Oaks, and they want to gaze upon the paths and by-ways where Scarlett and the Tarleton twins rode horseback in the lazy summer afternoons before the war clouds appeared above the peaceful tranquility of the old South.

In Atlanta it is the same. At the offices of the Atlanta Historical Society, with Miss Ruth Blair in charge, there are as many as one hundred requests a day from visitors for sightseeing trips throughout the city to spots made famous by Miss Mitchell's book.

They want to see Miss Pittypat's house. They want to see the Union Station where the wounded soldiers lay dying for want of medical attention. They want to see the exact site of the Battle of Atlanta, and to know if there are any breastworks left. Where was Scarlett's lumber mill? Where was the home of Scarlett and Rhett Butler? That of Ashley and Melanie? Belle Watling's on Decatur street? Peachtree and Marietta streets? Five Points?

Tara, Twelve oaks and the other houses and all the characters are fictional. Atlanta, Jonesboro, Peachtree, Five Points, Decatur and Marietta streets, the Union Station and the actions and events, however, are history. The people and the houses are typical of actual people and the houses of the period and the locality, but none of them are modeled after actual people and houses.

Georgia, however, is blessed in that there still remain many homes which are far-famed as the few remaining shrines of that gracious charm which history associates with the old South. In them that grand old tradition is still carried on. In them the present-day *Gone With The Wind* visitor sees the old South in its true manner and in the same way in which it was portrayed by Miss Mitchell in her book.

The old South lives again within the walls of these old homes and it is in them that visitors may vision the actions of the characters in *Gone With The Wind*. But it must be a mythical tour to Tara, to Twleve Oaks, and to Miss Pittypat's and to the other homes so often referred to in the book. In her extensive research work after acceptance of her book, Miss Mitchell went to considerable trouble to locate Tara at a point in the country where there was no house, and to locate Aunt Pittypat's house on what was a vacant lot during that period of the book.

As for the actual and historic sites mentioned in the book and regarding the movements of the army and the actions of the Yankee soldiers, and the sufferings of the Confederate soldiers, there is no doubt of their veracity. Diaries, histories and old newspapers support the latter as an everlasting contradiction to the flood of rumors which, unfortunately, have been rampant and have accumulated to the effect that the author overdescribed the desperate and devastating conditions which the South was forced to accept from the Northern armies.

That various points mentioned in the book bear authentic accuracy is evidenced by the fact that plans are now under way to place 70 to 100 temporary wooden markers on spots to commemorate the Battle of Atlanta. This action is a direct result of Miss Mitchell's book.

At the same time was outlined a concentrated program intended to bring about the placement eventually of 170 markers and the development of a history conscious citizenry.

Plans are under way to have itineraries for visitors whose interest in the city's historic sites has been aroused by the novel, and attractive folders presenting the city's history in brief form will be prepared, and policemen, especially, will be educated to direct visitors to the scenes of interest.

Since the publication of the book, Miss Mitchell has received thousands of letters and telephone calls from tourists who want to locate the battlefield of Peachtree Creek and other battles fought in and around Atlanta. Attendance at the Cyclorama, the painting of the Battle of Atlanta (July 22, 1864), has more than doubled. It is a work of historical, artistic and mechanical importance and is so in keeping and so appropriate with an important part of the book that even Atlantans are showing a revived interest in it.

The Mitchell home on Peachtree is one of the first places a visitor wants to see. It is the home of Eugene and Stephens Mitchell, father and brother of the author. The latter and her husband, John R. Marsh, public relations counsel of the Georgia Power Company, reside in an apartment a scant block away from the parental roof. Somehow the Mitchell home on Peachtree gives a breath of the old South, that fleeting atmosphere which vistors all want to feel. Southern mansions in and near Atlanta, including the famous Mimosa Hall in Roswell, have the mecca for tourists who desire to see a home with a real Southern appearance.

Tourists have been, and still are for that matter, coming to Atlanta by the thousands since Miss Mitchell's book was published, to familiarize themselves with the historic spots which have been so throroughly described by the author. They have motored to Georgia for that purpose. Cars bearing tags from the north, east, and west are almost articulate in their intent to tour the *Gone With The Wind* area.

Georgians, of course, are familiar with the scenes in the book, but it has nevertheless inspired these same Georgians to dig down into their history books for more accurate understanding and information in order to tell the world when she comes rolling in the State behind her steering wheel.

Jonesboro, in Clayton County, is the scene of part of the book, and the town has become the mecca for thousands of visitors looking for Tara and Twelve Oaks. And they all believe the famous old landmark (Tara) still stands, so vividly has Miss Mitchell painted it.

The publicity, the historic publicity, which Atlanta and Georgia have received from *Gone With The Wind* has been unparalleled in the annals of the State and has proved an inspiration and an information to millions. It has received the congratulations of the Georgia State Senate in a resolution unanimously adopted by the upper branch of the Assembly.

The resolution was signed by Senate President John Spivey and by Senators Atkinson of Savannah, Millican of Atlanta, McCutcheon of Dalton, and Williams of Waycross. Senator Atkinson, before asking the passing of the resolution, pointed out that it was the only major book in recent years which truly depicted the life of the South.

Miss Mitchell has done more than write a famous novel. By the historical background which she has presented she has brought to light many facts which, because of rumor and legend, have been accepted and confused as authentic and where haste and carelessness have resulted in serious misstatements.

Visitors to Georgia, supplied with guidebooks and a thirst for background for Scarlett and Rhett, Melanie and Ashley, and all the other characters and events, have only to get into their cars and begin to tour.

These tourists will see Georgia through the eyes of Scarlett O'Hara, who has risen to the top place in fictional history.

They will ride up and down Peachtree and live again in the days when the handsome and dashing Captain Rhett Butler rode horseback with his little daughter, Bonnie.

That same Peachtree stands today as one of the thoroughfares of the world. That same Georgia remains, of which Miss Mitchell wrote.

Margaret Mitchell-1937

Altanta, Ga.

January 26, 1937

To the members of the Annual Staff
and to the Students of Washington Seminary:

As measured by the years, it has been a long time since I was Literary Editor of the Washington Seminary Annual. But as measured by memory, it is only yesterday. That is the queer thing about growing older. The things which happened long ago are as close as the events of just last week — sometimes closer — for the memory of the work I did on the Annual Staff is as vivid as my labors on *Gone With The Wind*.

With this telescoping of time, it is not strange that I should feel very flattered, very elated, very humble that the 1937 Seminary Annual is dedicated to me. It is almost as if this honor had come to me while I was still wearing middy blouses and two large hair ribbons on my braids and speeding to school every morning on roller skates.

In *Gone With The Wind*, the old colored coachman, Uncle Peter, says warningly to Scarlett, "It ain' gwine do you no good ter stan' high wid de Yankees . . . ef yo' own folks doan 'prove of you." Thank you, "my own folks," for 'proving of me enough to dedicate this Annual to me.

MARGARET MITCHELL

McCLESKEY

Mrs. Thomas McCleskey the former Elizabeth Shewmake recalled a visit from Peggy Mitchell in 1938.

I had just become engaged to Doc. (her late husband, Dr. Thomas M. McCleskey) and Peggy called and said she wanted to come to see me: I was living in the home of my parents, Claude Shewmake and the late Mrs. Shewmake on West Peachtree Street just opposite the intersection of Eleventh Street.

One Afternoon in mid December, Peggy came by. It was a cold day and we were sitting in the den before a nice warm fire sipping hot tea.

Lilly Mae, the family maid kept coming in time after time putting logs on the fire.

Finally, Peggy said, "Is Lilly Mae trying to burn us up?"

Then, I called her and she came in and I told her we were about to burn up and for her not to bring any more logs in until I called her.

And Lilly Mae said, "No mam I won't but I was just so thrilled with how cute Miss Scarlett is."

Of course she had heard about *Gone With The Wind* and I had told her the *Gone With The Wind* lady was coming to see me.

When Peggy was ready to leave she went to the kitchen door and said, "Good bye Lilly Mae, the tea was grand and so were the little sandwiches you made. Now take care of Miss Elizabeth!"

Then Lilly Mae said, "Thank you so much Miss, can I walk you out to your car?"

Peggy told her yes and just before leaving she opened her very large handbag and brought out a large package — "Here's your trousseau present and I hope you will enjoy it."

The gift was a large brocade bag which has been a favorite accessory for Mrs. McCleskey when she goes partying.

ROOSEVELT

Former First Lady, Eleanor wrote a syndicated column tagged, "My Day during the 1930's." It ran in the Atlanta constitution.
In the following column the date line was Hyde Park, N.Y.

After I went to bed last night I started marking my mail, but I always end up by allowing myself time to read something I really enjoy.

For an hour I found myself deeply engrossed with the trials which the women who lived in Georgia suffered during the Civil War. *Gone With The Wind* is a book you would like to read straight through, but since there are so many things which have to be done, I can't. By reading it slowly you would perhaps enjoy it much better.

If you have not read it, I can assure you, you will find Scarlett O'Hara an interesting character. For pure selfishness and ruthlessness she seems to be almost incredible. But circumstances would even warrant the little animal she seems to be. But Scarlett and Rhett Butler are the two strongest and most interesting people. Scarlett was selfish to the end, but she did have gallantry, courage and determination.

In her rather strong way she did love two people in the course of her stormy existence. She paid in suffering for the fact that she never for one moment gave her love unselfishly. She never understood either the two men she loved and lost them both to be baffled and bitter in her loneliness.

I finished *Gone With The Wind* last night. It was written by Margaret Mitchell. It is a most interesting picture of the South during the "War Between The States," but to me the Reconstruction Period is far more interesting.

It is easy to understand why the women of the South kept their bitterness toward the Northern invaders. The war to them was a sacred cause and the actions of the North was practically impossible for them to understand.

Sometimes you hear people wonder today why the bitterness has persisted so long, but to me, it seems only natural and this book should help to make it vividly clear, even to those who hadn't understood it before.

The characters, Melanie and Ashely are very charming people that you would like to know. Scarlett and Rhett Butler are the two strongest and most interesting people.

So far, the remark of old Granny Fontaine, "That you should always keep something to fear and something to love in the world," is the wisest piece of psychology in the book.

GARRETT

Franklin Garrett, Atlanta's offical historian had the following comments and letters. The copies of the enclosed booklet covers are self explanatory.

The enclosed letter to me from Margaret indicates her displeasure when anyone attempted to give a specific location for any of the residences which formed a vital part of her book.

The other enclosure is a copy of the engraved invitation to Margaret's funeral. I have attended a lot of funerals, but do not remember any other where an invitation was necessary for attendance.

Atlanta Georgia

February 23,1939

Dear Franklin:

I have an embarrassing matter to take up with you, and I know of no other way of handling it except to dive right in.

Several days ago I noticed an item in the papers about the "See Atlanta First" Tour which will take place on February 24th. I noted with distress and a great sense of weariness that, among other points of interest which were to be visited, were the sites of the homes of my characters, "Aunt Pittypat, Rhett and Scarlett, Ashley and Melanie." My distress and weariness rose from the fact that for two and a half years I have spent most of my time telling people - by word of mouth, by letter, through the newspapers and over the radio - that my characters were completely fictional and so were their homes. There were no "sites" for my characters' homes. Because I did not wish the places to be identified, I went to great pains to mix up Atlanta geography. I studied old maps to make sure that even in my own mind I was locating houses where houses could not have stood. I went to as much pains about this as I did about the names of my characters, and it was a long and wearying affair. I had excellent reasons for not wishing the public to be able to say that "Scarlett lived here or there." I knew that if the rumor went about that Scarlett had lived upon a certain spot inevitably people would believe that the family who had lived on that spot in the sixties were Scarlett's family. That would be highly embarrassing to innocent people and to me too.

One of my greatest problems since *Gone With The Wind* was published has been the determination of tourists and many Atlanta people to identify such spots. I believe that I, and I alone, am the only person in the world who knows the truth about this matter, and if I say I had no definite sites in mind, then I am speaking the truth and everyone else is wrong. I have made this statement to the newspapers no less than a hundred times; people who have made radio talks about my book never failed to mention it; I have written hundreds of letters; and I have no count of the number of people whom I have told personally that neither the houses nor the sites of the houses of my characters existed.

So, you can understand my indignation and my sense of defeat when I read in the papers that the Atlanta Convention Bureau, which should know better, was busy adding and spreading and giving authenticity to these errors. As I was ill with a cold, John telephoned Faber Bollinger to find out why the Bureau was deliberately trying to embarrass me and to cause me even greater trouble from tourists than I have already had. Mr. Bollinger replied that he was very sorry, as such had not been their intent, and that the sites of the houses had been given to him by you. Coming as they did from the Vice President of the Atlanta Historical Society, Mr. Bollinger naturally thought he was getting accurate information. He said he would gladly eliminate these alleged points of interest from the tour, and regretted that the newspaper story had already gone out.

Franklin, I know you would not deliberately cause me any trouble, nor would you for worlds go on record with an inaccurate statement. So I am at a loss to understand why you included these nonexistent houses in a historical tour, especially in view of the two-year fight I have made in the papers on the subject. I do not doubt that to many people my feeling about this matter seems very strange. But I feel very deeply on the very subject, even as I do when people make flatfooted statements identifying characters in my book with actual people. When I went to so much trouble to keep this very thing from happening, it is disheartening to have friends make all my efforts go for nothing. I beg of you, in the future if anyone should ask you about where my characters lived, please say they lived only in my mind.

I am sorry to have to write this letter, but I know I'm in for another session of trouble, both from tourists and from the descendants of people who once lived on the sites you mentioned. So I thought I'd better write you frankly and tell you that I intend to lay the blame on you.

Sincerely,

Margaret Mitchell

Editor's Note: The handwritten letter from Mr. Garrett stated the misunderstanding was adjusted to Margaret Mitchell's entire satisfaction on February 29, 1939.

Mr. Garrett's Letter continues:

Following are two other little episodes that might be of interest:

On a Saturday afternoon in early 1936, Margaret Mitchell accompanied the late Messrs. Beverly M. DuBose, Sr., Wilbur G. Kurtz, Sr., and the current, Franklin M. Garrett, on a field trip. For many years past, DuBose, Kurtz and Garrett had been making field trips to locate cemeteries, Civil War battle fields, etc. On this particular Saturday, Margaret had expressed some interest in some Indian mounds on the Cobb County side of the Chattahoochee River, near Bolton. Enroute in Mr. DuBose's automobile, the subject of Margaret's forthcoming book came up. She had made the statement that she would be happy if it sold as many as a thousand copies.

The late De Sales Harrison served as President of the Piedmont Driving Club from 1938-1940. He was a close friend of mine and was responsible for my going with The Coca-Cola Company in 1940. Some time in 1939, Dee, who did not know the Marshes very well and knowing that I did know them and saw them occasionally, asked me to sound them out as to whether or not they would like to

Margaret Mitchell
and Her Novel

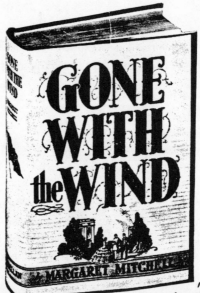

SEE page 19 — I hope you don't mind.
I never dreamed they'd use this. It
came from a personal letter I wrote
a friend at the Macmillan Co.
                              Margaret Mitchell Marsh

Cover of a booklet from the Macmillan Company.

Margaret Mitchell
and Her Novel

GONE WITH
THE WIND

*This booklet has been compiled
in response to a flood of requests from readers
all over the country for information
about the author and her book.*

THE MACMILLAN COMPANY
NEW YORK
1936

Title page of the booklet.

become members of the Driving Club. At that time, Margaret and John lived in the Della Manta Apartments at Piedmont Avenue and South Prado, diagonally across from the Driving Club tennis courts. I had occasion to visit Margaret and John at their apartment soon afterward and sounded them out and they would be pleased to become members of the club. I related this information to Dee and they were soon issued an invitation, which they promptly accepted.

Margaret and John were not interested in attending a lot of large social functions, but derived great pleasure from using the club for quiet luncheons. All they had to do was walk across the street. John remained a member until his death in 1952.

Whether any of the above is of interest in connection with your book, I do not know, but, at any rate, you are welcome to use any or all of it.

Frances joins me in affectionate regards.

Sincerely yours,

Franklin M. Garrett
Historian

Franklin Garrett.

Photo Section

Book & Movie
Era

Margaret just before publication of *Gone With The Wind*.

Margaret and her father, Eugene Mitchell, examining the first edition.

Margaret being interviewed by telephone for the
Associated Press.

Expressing her gratitude over WSB Radio for the
1937 Pulitzer Prize.

"The Dump," where Margaret wrote much of *Gone With The Wind.*

The Della Manta, where Margaret lived
from 1939 to 1949.

A plaque in memory of Margaret at the
Della Manta, now called One South Prado.

Margaret was an avid reader and a meticulous researcher.

Four of the 27 translations of *Gone With The Wind* — Swedish, German and two Dutch editions.

And then came the movie. Opening night at Loew's Grand Theater.

Margaret arriving.

Clark Gable and Margaret meet.

Clark Gable and Vivien Leigh.

Rhett creates antagonism in a scene in the movie.

Rhett and Scarlett escape from burning Atlanta.

First premier of *Gone With The Wind*. L to R Margaret Mitchell, John Marsh, Clark Gable, Carole Lombard and Atlanta Mayor William B. Hartsfield.

Margaret and John Marsh at the second premier in 1940.

The Man — Clark Gable as Rhett The Woman — Vivien Leigh as Scarlett

MRS. R.C. HUNT

Members of the Atlanta Women's Press Club gave a large cocktail party at the Piedmont Driving Club in the afternoon of the world premiere of the movie of Gone With The Wind Dec. 15, 1939 at the Loew's Grand Theater.

Guests attending were the stars in the movie who had come to Atlanta for the world premiere and VIP's of the press and MGM who made the film.

Mrs. Robert C. Hunt, the former Elizabeth Whitman of Atlanta, was a long-time news and social writer for the Hearst owned Georgian-American, was vice president of the Press Club, and she recalls the following:

Peggy stayed in the ladies' lounge until all the movie stars and VIP's arrived. However, several times, wearing dark glasses, she would sneak out and ask one of us: "Has Mr. Gable arrived?"

He finally arrived with his wife, Carole Lombard. Later he (Rhett Butler) and Vivien Leigh (Scarlett O'Hara) met Peggy for the first time. A photo was made of the trio and came out the next morning on the front page of the Atlanta *Constitution*. It was one of the most exciting events of the weekend.

Later, Mrs. Hunt worked for the Red Cross in Atlanta, and recalled this incident:

It was in 1942 and the Red Cross had set up a coffee room and a sewing room in the chapter house of the Joseph Habersham Chapter of the Daughters of the American Revolution, located on 15th Street and Piedmont Avenue directly across from the Piedmont Driving Club.

Peggy was doing volunteer work for the Red Cross and came by daily and also did some "homework," said Mrs.Hunt. "Things like sewing buttons on uniforms and shirts of the soldiers." Many hundreds of soldiers were in camp, set up in nearby Piedmont Park.

Many of them came over just for a glimpse of the noted author of *Gone With The Wind*. All were very polite and well mannered when Peggy served them coffee and doughnuts.

December 16, 1939
The Atlanta *Journal and Constitution*

PETITE ATLANTAN MEETS FILM STARS FOR THE FIRST TIME

The man who put $4,000,000 into filming *Gone With The Wind* and the principal stars who put their hearts into it, met the author of the book for the very first time yesterday afternoon.

Petite Margaret Mitchell, quiet of voice, smiling somewhat reservedly, gave her hand to David O. Selznick, the producer: to Clark Gable, Vivien Leigh, Evelyn Keys, Ann Rutherford and Laura Hope Crews, of the cast and to Carole Lombard, Gable's glamorous wife, at a cocktail party of the Atlanta Women's Press Club.

Said Mr. Gable: "Do you suppose I could have a few words with her? After all there is a lot I want to ask her."

Said Margaret Mitchell: "Isn't he grand! Just what I expected."

Said Carole Lombard: "Clark has been dying to meet you, Miss Mitchell."

Miss Vivien Leigh: "I think she is perfectly marvelous."

It all took place in a room 18x11. There was another room and the bar, into which quests overflowed.

Peggy Mitchell had the spotlight and stole the scene. The greatest names of Hollywood gave it to her willingly.

Gable only wanted to talk to "Peggy" Mitchell, and Gable, as in all his movie roles, found a way to get his girl.

They dissappeared into a private dining room of the club at 5:16 o'clock. The door was locked. There Gable and Miss Mitchell talked over many things. Both refused to repeat what was said. The world would like to know the things they talked about but probably never will.

Minutes slipped by, but "Peggy" and "Rhett" were still in conference. The clock showed 5:25. Most of the club members were getting a little nervous. What were they saying? Was she telling him she had him in mind for her character when she wrote the book?

When they came out Peggy joined Vivien Leigh and Laura Hope

(Aunt Pittypat) Crews in the main room. She confided to them:

"If I sit up too straight, think nothing of it. Somebody jerked a chair back too far today and I sat down too hard on the floor. Now I'm wrapped in adhesive tape."

Carole Lombard slipped into a chair beside her.

Soon Miss Mitchell's husband, John Marsh, beckoned it was time to leave.

It was nearing 6 o'clock. Louis B. Mayer slipped her coat on for her. Mrs. Mayer was there and good byes were said. The guests were leaving. Miss Mitchell gave a farewell wave to Mr. and Mrs. Gable, who left by the side terrace entrance. Miss Mitchell left by the front door.

Claudette Colbert remained to entertain the guests.

"I hate to leave all this. Did Miss Mitchell have to leave so soon? Does she come to all the press club parties? Is she always as friendly as she was tonight?" asked Miss Colbert.

The crowd drank the remaining mint juleps.

Among the guests were Mrs. Selznick, Jock Whitney, Laurence Olivier, Ona Munson, Miss Alicia Rhett, Louis B. Mayer, Robert Samuels, Mrs. Sidney Howard, John F. Wharton, Mr. and Mrs. Daniel T. O'Shea, W.R. Ferguson, Mr. and Mrs. E.B. Coleman, Mr. and Mrs. Herbert Bayard Swope, Mr. and Mrs. Charles Payson, Mr. and Mrs. Robert Lehman, Mr. and Mrs. Barklie Henry, Mr. and Mrs. Howard Dietz, Howard Strickling, Major and Mrs. Lenox R. Lohr, W.F. Rodgers, T.J. Connors.

Mr. and Mrs. James Barrett, Mr. and Mrs. George Brett Jr., Mr. and Mrs. R.M. Brett, H.S. Lathem, Mr. and Mrs. A.J. Blanton, Mr. and Mrs. Allan Taylor, Miss Susan Myrick, Mrs. Julia Peterkin, Miss Inez Robb, Miss Marjorie Kinnan Rawlings, former Governor and Mrs. James M. Cox, Mr. and Mrs. James M. Cox Jr.

W.S. Kirkpatrick, Nate Noble and John Paschal, godfathers of the club; Mrs. W.S. Kirkpatrick, Mrs. Nate Noble, Mr. and Mrs. Wilbur Kurtz, Mr. and Mrs. Stephens Mitchell, Mr. and Mrs. Norman Berg, Mr. and Mrs. Lucien Harris Jr., Miss Margaret Baugh, John A. Brice; Major and Mrs. Clark Howell, Mr. and Mrs. Randolph A. Hearst and Eddie Pentecost.

Sunday Dec. 14, 1975
The Atlanta *Journal and Constitution*

AUTHOR'S COAT HANGS IN HALL

By YOLANDE GWIN
On Dec. 15 in Thirty Nine,
Atlantans and stars were all in line;
Hardly a star is now alive;
But Atlantans remember in seventy-five.

Yes, many Atlantans can think back to Dec. 15, 1939, for that was the date of one of the most spectacular events in Atlanta's history.

It was the world premiere of the movie version of Margaret Mitchell's *Gone With The Wind* one of the world's greatest books.

Thousands jammed the streets in front of Loew's Grand Theater. Huge spotlights shot their rays in zig-zag fashion over the thousands who stood outside on Peachtree Street and what is now Margaret Mitchell Square.

The diminutive young author arrived for the festivities with her husband John Marsh, wearing a full length oyster white velvet coat with all over embroidery of gold and silver metallic threads interwoven in an effect design. She was greeted by many of the city's dignitaries including the late Mayor William B. Hartsfield and he late Julian Boehm. Peggy also wore a tiny white bow in her short cropped hair.

That coat, given many years later to the Atlanta Historical Society, is now on exhibit in the new and currently open museum in the James M. Cox Room at the new McElreath hall on the Atlanta Historical Society compound.

Prior to its present location it was on display at the Swan House, home of the society.

The evening of the *Gone With The Wind* premiere topped the events of that fabulous period. Top stars of the movie, plus MGM officials, (the movie producers) invaded the city, and there were many parties preceding the premiere, as well as afterwards, given for them. One of the largest was the Junior League *Gone With The Wind* costume ball at the City Auditorium. Mrs. W. Colquitt Carter was the League President that year.

Margaret Palmer, daughter of Mrs. Charles Palmer and the late Mr. Palmer, was chosen among many prominent young belles of the time, to wear the dress that "Scarlett" wore in one of the movie scenes. She led the grand march with Clark Gable.

At the Atlanta Women's Press Club party at the Piedmont Driving Club for Miss Mitchell, (who was a press club member) and for the stars like Rhett Butler (Gable), Scarlett O'Hara (Vivien Leigh), Carole Lombard, who was married to Gable at the time, Laurence Olivier, who was "courting" Miss Leigh at the time, Olivia de Haviland and many more was a tremendous affair.

The parade from the airport (when the stars arrived) through town and on out Peachtree Street to the Georgian Terrace Hotel, (the stars stayed there) was one of the largest ever held here. At that time, the police estimated the crowd that lined Peachtree to see the stars (all riding in open cars) as more than the combined armies of Generals Sherman, Johnson and Hood during the Atlanta campaign in 1864.

At one of the parties, Gable said that he had heard that there were over 300,00 people in Atlanta. He also said:

"When I saw all those people even the young ones, who had climbed up on telephone and electric poles, and those leaning out office windows, it seemed to me like three million. Everybody was waving and cheering. It was really one of the most exciting moments of my life. And Miss Mitchell, my, she is a real wonderful lady."

TWELVE OAKS

Twelve Oaks, the home of Ashley Wilkes, in *Gone With The Wind's* book and movie is the real thing, not "reel" thing.

Yes, it was an inspiration, but it still sits in Southern splendor, a gracious remnant of a glorious past.

The sweet scent of Magnolia drifts across the veranda, sprawling fields shimmer under the Georgia sun while katydids sing summer songs. . . . suddenly you are right there with Rhett and Scarlett and Prissy, too.

Now, it is Lovejoy Plantation, home of Betty Talmadge. It was built in 1836, most of the original structure is just as it was before the Civil War. The home is grandly decorated with antiques and memorabilia of its history.

The property was bought by Thomas Crawford in 1835. The plantation home was built with hand hewn timbers, the interior woodwork is of Georgia Heart Pine. There are six fluted columns in the front, which support a broad, two story porch with a long hanging balcony on the second floor. The farm consists of 1200 acres.

The region was made famous first in military maneuvers during the Atlanta campaign of the Civil War. Then of course it became a part of Margaret Mitchell's *Gone With The Wind*.

Legend says that when Yankees approached Lovejoy's Station on the Macon Georgia and Western Railroad, Crawford filled the tall porch columns with grain to prevent it from being captured by the enemy. The lawns of Lovejoy Plantation were the scene of a battle between Confederate and Northern soldiers, mini-balls were discovered in the walls of the home of Mrs. Talmadge, during restoration.

Battle trenches may still be seen within a mile of the home.

Lovejoy Plantation is only a short distance from the spot where Confederate General Hood paused to regroup his remaining forces after the ill-fated Battle of Atlanta. When Hood's forces went forth from Lovejoy, they left Georgia to face the last devastation of Sherman's March to the sea.

One long-ago lady of the house is said to have fired, from the stairway, down on a Yankee deserter who had come to plunder.

Beauty, serenity, history, and the true Old South, Lovejoy Plantation has been chosen for entry in the National Register. It is open year round to special groups by appointment only.

Mrs. Talmadge has the facade of the movie version of Tara in *Gone With The Wind*. She has it stored in a secret place awaiting restoration.

She also has the fictional Tara, the old Fitzgerald house, a ramshackle, five room place that once belonged to Miss Mitchell's grandparents. Mrs. Talmadge paid $1,000 for it and moved it five miles to her farm, like Tara, to be restored.

The Old Fitzgerald House.

HARWELL

Richard Harwell of Washington, Georgia has a large collection of Gone With The Wind's *history as well as books he himself has written on the same subject.*

The following concerns the film:

One of the big problems in filming Gone With The Wind, was to have Tara look exactly like Margaret Mitchell wrote it. MGM, the producers had to really make out boxwood and oak leaves out of fine paper.

There were no trees in Hollywood that resembled Georgia trees. So the behind-the-camera workers used large poles, like telephone poles, placed on the ground around Tara. Of course the Tara you have seen in the movie and on postcards and magazines was only the front of the house. Indoor scenes were made in the various studios on the set.

When the telephone poles were placed on Tara's property which we see on Tara's yard, ribs were added to the poles to make the diameter larger. Then over this was chicken wire and the bark was made of plaster. The ground and walkways were made to look like Georgia, two thousand loads of brick dust was poured over it.

Two real Magnolia trees were gotten and transplanted on Tara's property. The property department had to make thousands of dogwood leaves and these were pinned on the artificial trees.

Because the film officials had not found the right actress to be Scarlett, the filming was begun on schedule for the other parts of the movie. The first shot was when Atlanta was burning by you know who. A stand-in for Clark Gable (Rhett Butler), who was trying to get the horse and wagon away from the smoke and flames which were coming from the ammunition warehouses and railroad boxcars.

Additional quotes from Richard Harwell:

By informing readers about the American Civil War, it convinced Europeans that the United States had a history of its own.

The extent of the history in Gone With The Wind is deceptive. There is a little of military history. It is history of the little things of life — how women made hats of cornshucks, buttons from seed, food from wild plants (even from leaves), how they nursed wounded soldiers and how they held up the morale of the Confederacy even past the sticking point. This homely history is the history of which Margaret Mitchell was an unmatched master.

The rarest American edition of *Gone With The Wind* is that produced for the dedication of WSB's "White Columns on Peachtree" in April 1956. Only five hundred copies were issued. They were bound in brown skiver leather, gold stamped and included a frontispiece showing an artist's rendering of the WSB building.

Margaret Mitchell did not take to fame. She resisted it as well as she could. It overtook her. It overwhelmed her. She became a virtual prisoner of her own fame.

When Sam Tupper Jr., reviewed *Gone With The Wind* for the Atlanta *Journal*, June 28, 1936 he concluded:

"It is not too much to say that *Gone With The Wind* is among the most powerful and original novels in American literature. With its scope, its high emotion and shrewd picturization, it is a book to own and to re-read and remember forever."

Ouside of writing, Peggy Michell liked to tell or listen to a good story. She had the gift of dramatic exaggeration which could make the story better in the telling. One of her best was by resentful young people about an Atlanta grande dame of a generation ago, who was frequently calling upon the young people to do a lot of free work for her parties.

Those who heard Peggy tell that story can almost see and hear her now as she said, "They all decided they'd fix that old lady. So when she was putting on a big garden party at which a lot of the young folks had to put on some sort of acts..." First came up the fire engines, saying, "Where is the fire?" They just got shooed off when up came a hearse, the driver asked: "Where is the corpse?" They just backed down the drive when up came the paddy wagon with the cops shouting, "Where is the riot?" And when the poor old sister, who was about to faint by then, got rid of the cops, up came a wagon from the pest house, the driver asked, "Where are the people with the small pox?"

That fixed her all right — the young folks never had any more trouble.

These sketches are from Brooks-Van Horne Costumes in New York City. They were given to Yolande by the late Stephens Mitchell, brother of Peggy.

PIKE

Mrs. J. Sanders Pike, the former Mary Upshaw wrote the following after being asked if she knew Margaret Mitchell.
The following is an autograph from Miss Mitchell to Dr. Upshaw:

For Dr. C.B. Upshaw-
In the hope that he will look with tolerance on the obstetrics and gynecology practiced within these pages.

With Affection

margaret mitchell

My father, Dr. Charles Bell Upshaw, Sr. was Margaret Mitchell's personal physician and operated on her two times. My first recollection of her name was on an evening in 1936 when father said we all had to gather by the radio and listen to the 6 o'clock news when his patient was going to be interviewed by Medora Field Perkerson about her new book.

In 1939 just before the premiere of Gone With The Wind in Atlanta, Margaret Mitchell took an old costume of a red gingham dress with a white apron, pantaloons, and a white bonnet to my father for me to wear to the ball to be held the night before the premiere.

The day before the premiere she was at a luncheon at the Piedmont Driving Club and someone pulled the chair out from under her and she sat on the floor. She had to go to my father's office where he strapped her back up. She gave him an old fashioned bouquet for me to carry to the premiere.

After the premiere I had it framed into a tray and he asked her to sign it. She refused as she had given up autographing. So when one of his brothers died and she wrote him a sympathy note, I cut her signature off and put it with the framed bouquet.

He operated on her at Piedmont Hospital shortly after the premiere and all the hospital doctors and nurses went into her room to see her which upset her terribly. When she had to be operated on again a few years later, she requested to go to the St. Joseph's Hospital so the Nuns could take care of her. She told my father her reasons and he assured her he could control the people coming into her room if she would just go to Piedmont. She agreed and this proved to be very successful. My father would visit her each morning and she had a coffee pot in her room and they would have a cup of coffee together. When he had to make a house visit he would have to call her apartment and speak to her maid to tell her he was coming so she would open the door.

For several years during the war I worked with her at the old SAE House (Ga. Tech) which was used by the Red Cross for rolling bandages. She and I served in the food line.

Recently, while in Charleston I found out that she had joined the Huguenot Society of South Carolina in 1930 under the Munnerlyn French name which was her middle name. This was unusual in the thirties for a Catholic to join such a society. She was married first to an Upshaw but never mentioned this to my father.

In August 1949, my father and I were returning from France on the Ile de France. Each morning they put out a one page bulletin of world events and one morning they published the fact that Margaret Mitchell had been hit by a taxi and was in critical condition in Atlanta. Each day after that they had a short paragraph about her. My father sent a cable from the ship to Grady which read "Seven Atlantans* aboard are all thinking about you." This was printed in the *Atlanta Journal.*

*The seven were Dr. Charles Bell Upshaw, Mary Upshaw, Mr. and Mrs. Otis Barge, Dorothy Barge, and Mr. and Mrs. Frank Spratlin.

MANGHAM

This column was one of a group of former governors interviewed for a
series on Georgia's former governors by Yolande Gwin which appeared in the
Atlanta Journal and Constitution *during 1974.*

Mrs. J.J. Mangham, Jr. of Breman Ga. is the daughter of former Georgia
Governor E.D. Rivers and Mrs. Rivers of Lakeland, Ga. Rivers was governor
from 1937 to 1947 and he and Mrs. Rivers lived in the official Governor's
mansion in Atlanta's Ansley Park.

Mrs. Mangham the former Jerry Rivers said that one of her most cherished
possessions is her scrapbook on Gone With The Wind *book as well as the*
movie.

One of the highlights of our time at the mansion was the premiere
of *Gone With The Wind.* We had a tea at the mansion for the movie
stars and the visiting dignitaries and they were all gracious and
charming. I shall never forget Carol Lombard's complete devotion to
her husband, Clark Cable.

She lost sight of him momentarily when the large number of
people greeting him separated them. She turned to me and said,
"Oh, where is he? I don't see Clark." I finally spotted him with a
group of people and she said, "Isn't he wonderful? Oh, I must be
close to him."

Later I went into the kitchen and there was Carol and Clark
talking to the cook, butler and maid. Clark was overheard asking the
cook what she was taking out of the oven. When he was told it was
cornbread, Clark immediately asked for a piece buttered and said he
much preferred it to the canapes.

At the premiere Vivien Leigh sat with Mother and Dad, and my
husband and I sat behind them. I noticed Miss Leigh crying and my
mother comforting her. Later I asked Mother why she was crying,
Mother said Miss Leigh was afraid people would be disappointed in
her in the movie!

HITT, SR.

Mrs. Edward G. Hitt, Sr. is the former Lamar Slaton, daughter of the late Mr. and Mrs. William Martin Slaton.

They, the latter couple, and Mr. and Miss Eugene Mitchell were friends, as well as neighbors on Jackson Street in Atlanta. Mr. Mitchell was president of the Atlanta Board of Education as well as the father of Margaret Mitchell; Mr. Slaton, as his father, the late Major William Franklin Slaton, was the Superintendent of the Atlanta Public Schools.

Mrs. Hitt, Sr. remembers Peggy Mitchell telling her the following after each were grown ladies:

As a child I always thought your mother was a witch — because every time she would come over to sit on our front porch to visit she would say: "I think there is a cat lurking around here, and every time a cat would appear."

Mrs. Hitt, Sr. thinks her mother is allergic to cats and that Peggy was eight years old at the time. An example of her vivid imagination she says.

Atlanta

June 23, 1944

Dear Lamar:

It was sweet of you and Ned to send the beautiful vase of flowers. The splashes of yellow and purple are still brightening the apartment. We have always felt happy in the long friendship between your family and ours. When I saw you the day of the funeral, I suddenly remembered a much earlier day when your father and mine were mounting horses to inspect the building of new schools and to confound the unrighteous who wished to pay more for schools than they thought necessary. I found that memory very comforting.

Margaret Mitchell Marsh

HITT, JR.

Mrs. Edward G. Hitt, Jr., the former Margaret Peavy, received the following letter from Margaret Mitchell:

Atlanta, Georgia

November 1, 1941

Dear Margaret:

I recall from my own debut days that corsages had a habit of coming in bunches. They died in the refrigerator before they could all be worn. Then there were stretches when there were no corsages at all, and these periods always coincided with a very important party, and, worse luck, with the time the family decided that if they were buying dancing slippers and evening dresses they certainly weren't going to buy flowers too. So, if at any time this season you should be fresh out of orchids, call Harper's Colonial Flower Shop, on Peachtree at Twelfth, and tell them you want the flowers I have ordered for you. Let them know whether you'd rather have them for your hair or to wear on your shoulder or to carry.

You looked so beautiful at the Halloween Ball last night that it was a pleasure to watch you. I hope you have a very happy season.

Peggy Mitchell Marsh

This letter was on Peggy's personal stationery.

The following memorabilia illustrates one side of Margaret Mitchell's character that has never been public chit chat.

Mrs. E. G. Hitt, Jr. is the daughter of the late Mrs. Kitty Poole, who was a society and news reporter on the Atlanta Journal *during the 30's and 40's. Mrs. Poole tells this:*

Many flying cadets of the British Royal Air Force were in training in Macon, Ga. in 1942. Many weekend leaves were spent in Atlanta. Atlantans, in their usual Southern hospitality style, had several of the cadets as house guests. "Kitty," known as Mrs. Poole, always had some in her home.

Peggy and John Marsh lived in an apartment and didn't have room for overnight guests, but Peggy managed to do something for them.

Every week she wrote the parents of each cadet in England giving them happy news of their sons and how Atlantans loved them. This was a very thoughtful and also an affectionate gesture on her part — few knew of her letter writing.

After their training in Macon, the cadets returned to England for active duty.

This story does not have a happy ending. Each cadet was killed in action.

Just think how cherished those letters are that Peggy wrote for the parents, of the happy days their sons had in Georgia.

Mrs. E.G. Hitt, Jr.

SIBLEY

To Yolande Gwin from Celestine Sibley:

The Atlanta Women's Press Club was still a flourishing organization when I came to Atlanta in 1941. It met regularly, forswearing business meetings and solemn speeches in favor of jolly cocktail sessions, and all the women employed on the staffs of the *Constitution* and the *Journal* attended regularly and joyfully.

Yolande Gwin invited me to my first meeting, which was held at the Henry Grady Hotel. As we walked up Forsyth Street together I asked Yolande if there was a chance I'd get to meet the celebrated Miss Mitchell.

"Oh, of course," said Yolande. "Peggy will be there. She always comes to the meetings."

We were a little late and the meeting was in full swing with laughing chattering groups deployed around the cocktail table. Somebody wanted to talk to Yolande and bore her off before she could introduce the newcomer around, so I wandered about on my own. A plump little woman in a funny Carmen Miranda style hat recognized that I was a stranger and promptly engaged me in conversation. She talked about books and newspapering and blackouts which had just been instituted to save Atlanta from German bombers. She herself was an air raid warden in the blocks surrounding the Piedmont Driving Club, she said.

She made a funny story of her adventures, telling me that her co-captain in the neighborhood was Julius Gaines, the highly respected black headwaiter at the Driving Club. I remarked that I lived in the area and was going to have to leave pretty soon to catch the Piedmont-Morningside bus.

"Oh, don't bother with the bus," she said. "I have my car and I'm going, too. I'll give you a ride."

"Thank you," I said. "Let me go make my manners to Yolande and get my coat."

Yolande was surrounded, but I got close enough to thank her and to tell her I was leaving and murmur, "I wish I'd had a chance to meet Margaret Mitchell. Is she here?"

"Well, you've been talking to her all evening," said Yolande. The plump little woman in the fuuny hat was my ride home, my neighbor, and one of the most gracious people I ever met.

Margaret Mitchell.

Celestine Sibley.

LOCKERMAN

From Doris Lockerman to Yolande Gwin:

When my husband, Allen Lockerman and our two sons were preparing to move to Atlanta in 1942, John Shinnick, a colleague of mine on the *Chicago Tribune* mentioned that I must look them up when we got settled.

By that time, Margaret Mitchell had long been a world celebrity and it was well known that she fled from intrusion of every sort. I gave no thought to John's suggestion.

Soon after I signed on as a reporter at the Atlanta *Journal*, I met Peggy at several meetings of the Atlanta Women's Press Club, where she was at ease with her journalist friends, many of whom were old associates on the Atlanta newspapers and Atlanta *Journal* magazine.

After a few months, she telephoned Allen and me, and invited us to go to see "Heavenbound," the traditional dramatic parable produced at Big Bethel Church. It had long been recognized as a spectacular and polished production and the Marshes were strong and avid supporters. "You will be enchanted," Peggy told us.

We were. When the performance had ended I asked them casually if they happened to know John Shinnick at the *Chicago Tribune*. They exploded with laughter. Shinnick, it seems, had been a college friend of John Marsh's and he had written them a long note about us. When I did not call, nor mention him after a few meetings, they realized that we did not intend to engage the long-distance introduction. They set a bet between themselves on whether we would ever acknowledge it.

One of Peggy's off-beat interests was a class in writing she had established for inmates at the Federal Penitentiary. She soon learned she needed someone to alternate with her as a teacher and she asked if I would help her. The Program was well underway but I accepted and found an over-flowing room of convicts, fully aware of who Margaret Mitchell was, and eager to improve their writing skills from one of the foremost authors in the world.

An Afternote: At least one of the students reportedly became a successful colunmist for a west coast newspaper after his release from the penitentiary.

Doris Lockerman

HASTINGS

Mrs. Donald Hastings (Louise) of Lovejoy (just outside Atlanta), said at her estate "Floweracres":

Margaret was such a private person that I felt it was a privilege to know her, as I did. Of course she was Peggy to me.

When *Gone With The Wind* was selected as the Book of the Month, at the review the chairman asked Margaret Mitchell to make a speech.

Margaret Mitchell said, "Mrs. Morrison, you know I cannot make a talk but I feel like what Mammie said, 'It don't do no good for the Yankee soldiers to love you if your own don't,' so it doesn't do any good for the Yankees to love my book unless you do."

Margaret Mitchell was asked to be one of the speakers on Authors Night at the National Council of State Garden Clubs meeting held in Atlanta during World War II.

Margaret Mitchell said, "I don't know why Louise asked me to speak at a garden club meeting. I can kill a mother-in-law's tongue in two days."

Margaret worked tirelessly with the Red Cross during the war years.

CARY WILMER, JR.

Cary Wilmer, Jr. is the son of the late Rev. Cary Wilmer, Rector of St. Luke's Episcopal Church in Atlanta from 1900 to 1924. Mrs. Wilmer, Jr. of Atlanta saved many letters to him from Margaret Mitchell while he was serving in the U.S. Air Force, beginning in Roswell, New Mexico in December 1942 and ending with his honorable discharge from Lowry Field in Denver, Colorado in 1945.

The Piedmont Driving Club on Piedmont Avenue is a posh social club where the city's most outstanding events take place.

Peggy and John Marsh lived one block — walking distance from the club to their apartment (the Della Manta) on South Prado in Ansley Park where many socialites lived at the time and also the Georgia Governors' mansion was there for many years.

After Peggy's death, John Marsh had a heart attack — yet very often he would stroll over to the nearby Piedmont Driving Club to have brunch with Cary Wilmer.

One Saturday they decided to go to a movie on Monday evening. The picture was Kind Hearts and Coronets, *starring Alec Guiness. It was his first American picture: Marsh in leaving the club stated that he was going to stay in bed all day Sunday.*

Monday morning Mr. Wilmer called Mr. Marsh to find out what time he could pick him up to go to the movie.

When he called, a woman answered the phone and when Mr. Wilmer asked to speak to Mr. Marsh she said, "He died last night Mr. Wilmer."

The following letters are from Margaret Mitchell to Mr. Wilmer.

January 4, 1943

Dear Cary:

It was good to hear from you and to know that after your long wait you had really arrived in the army and, what is more important, arrived at Roswell. It has seemed strange to go to the Driving Club for four o'clock lunches and not to find you there. Last night, Julius * asked about you, so I took it upon myself to tell him your special regards. Julius was so pleased about this and said he was very happy that you got into the service as you wished. "He had just sat around here so long, unable to do anything because he was waiting, that I was afraid he'd get plumb disgusted."

Sam Tupper ** was home for a New Year's furlough and I had

him and his mother and Medora Perkerson *** for lunch. All three
sent their very best regards to you.

I am feeling so old that I firmly believe I am the first white child
born in Fulton County. This season's Debutante Club decided to
have only one party. All thirty-eight of them and their mamas were
ranged round the wall of the Driving Club ballroom. As everyone in
town was invited and it was raining, the traffic was blocked from
Morningside to Tenth Street to the Christain Science Chruch. To
complicate matters, the jeeps and tanks of the Army War Show
camped in Piedmont Park were trying to get up the hill and across
Piedmont Avenue. There were no traffic policemen and when a
military policemen started to open a path an Atlanta dowager, who
shall be nameless, simply looked at him and he went off and never
returned. As such hordes of people had been invited, hundreds
were bidden from three to four o'clock, other hundreds from four
to five, and apparently thousands from five to six. It took an hour
and forty-four minutes by actual timing to get around the receiving
line, so it worked out that the entire guest list tried to get into the
club at the same time. I was fatigued from three weeks of mending
soldiers' clothes and felt old enough from that, and when I saw that
the first debutante was the daughter of a girl of my own debut year I
felt gray hairs quickening on my scalp. To add to the horror of the
situation, the next two debs were daughters of women who came
out several years after I did. Feeling very cheerless, I made my weary
way to the soft couch in the dining room and discovered a swarm of
Club members who either had not been bidden to the debut party
or who were strong-minded enough to resist invitations. They were
screaming around the bassinet of a lusty male infant who looked as if
he could handle a double Scotch with more ease than his bottle. I
inquired the identity of the infant and discovered that it was
Benjamin Mart Bailey, III. Then indeed did my decrepit old bones
rattle, for I had attended the wedding of the grandparents of this
baby. It is true I was the youngest wedding guest and it was my first
wedding and I distinguished myself on the occasion by getting loose
in a bowl of champagne punch and being distressingly ill behind a
rosewood sofa, but the fact remains that I had been present at the
grandparents' wedding. I do not think I will ever be any older than I
was at that moment.

If I can find any of those horrible things you smoke, I will keep you supplied. That's a fine way to speak of your generosity on Sunday afternoons, isn't it? I miss you and I hope you have good luck and do not have to sit around interminably for further training. After all, you've done your share of sitting around. Good luck and let us hear from you.

Best from John and me,

Peggy

* Julias Gaines began as a bus boy at the Driving Club and ended up as Maître d'.

** Sam Tupper is an Atlantan and member of the Driving Club.

*** Medora Field Perkerson was a close friend of Peggy and also author of *Who Killed Aunt Maggie?* and also *White Columns in Georgia.*

Atlanta, Georgia

January 26, 1943

Dear Cary:
It was good to have that long letter from you and I was glad to learn that, in spite of your "advanced age" and "physical infirmities", you were officially in the glider corps. The army certainly doesn't mind how they throw words around, and the statement about men who have reached the "advanced age of thirty-eight" is guaranteed to make any man feel as old as if he were the first white child born in Fulton County. It must have been disconcerting to discover that you had to stand a physical all over again when you thought that part lay behind you. More power to you that you passed and that you got in in spite of the Metheuseleh-like quantity of your years.

John grinned when he read the "shortage of office force" had moved you up to the "pass department," because in his war and in his outfit he was the only person who could work a typewriter and he was excused from cleaning the gents' room in order to make out papers in quadruplicate. He says there are worse things.

Now that the driving-for-pleasure restriction* has shown its teeth, there are not too many people at the Driving Club in the late afternoons. For a while it looked as if John and I, Esmond Brady and Mary Nelson Ream were going to have to uphold the morale for the entire membership, as we are almost the only members who live in walking distance. You cannot imagine the pathetic and beaming pleasure with which the colored staff greets Mary and me when we stop by for a Coca-Cola while we discuss Civilian Defense. Julius and Will and Mackey ** practically hover over us in order not to miss a single word, as though they were shipwrecked mariners having their first and only contact with civilization. Will told me that this was not like that other war, no ma'am, folks hadn't lost the use of their legs then and weren't too proud to ride the street cars, and, befo' God, there was more money and more rich folks and the Government hadn't taken all their cash and they certainly were big-hearted and open-handed. (At this, delicate hint, I gave him a dime.

As soon as one job stops another starts and, as usual, there is never a dull moment in the Marsh family. I'd no sooner brushed off the mud of the Army War Show and rid myself of the needle marks from mending soldiers' uniforms than the news came of the sinking of the "Atlanta." The campaign to sell enough bonds to build a new cruiser got under way immediately and, as sponser of the late lamented vessel, I found myself in the midst of the hullabaloo. This is one of the few money-raising campaigns I've ever seen in which almost all types of people participate. It is cheering and heartening to face a large women's rally and see presidents of organizations on the South Side check-by-jowl with the Pace's Ferry Roaders. Both papers have been squarely behind the campaign and the publicity has been extraordinarily good. With over ten million dollars raised and six weeks to go, we hope for success.

Hervey Allen, author of *Anthony Adverse*, has taken over the office of War Men Power — or is it Power War Man? Thus far, I understand, he has the job and the title but no office or telephone, which shows that the war on this front is proceeding in an encouragingly normal manner. I've never met Mr. Allen, although I have had letters from him and a phone conversation the other day, but I know him quite well through Bill Howland, who sees him whenever *Time* sends him to Miami. Mr. Allen sounds like a grand person and he and John and I are going to have dinner together soon. Years ago there used to be a saying that if you sat in a certain sidewalk cafe in Paris everyone in the world would eventually pass by. I never believed that about Paris, but it is true about Atlanta. Everyone you have ever heard of or read of eventually comes to Atlanta. I've never understood why people rushed off to New York or Paris "to meet interesting people"; if they'd just stay home in Atlanta, the interesting people would swamp them and Atlantans would save the wear and tear of travel. Ambassador Grew is the next on our program, for he will be here soon.

When you get time write and let us know what is happening to you. You know we'll be interested in any news.

Best to you from us both,

Peggy

* Driving for pleasure restriction in Atlanta was due to shortage of gas. It was wartime.

** Mackey was a car attendant at the Driving Club. Will was one of the bartenders.

Atlanta, Georgia

March 17, 1943

Dear Cary:

I do not see why you should permit Mr. Marion Hargrove to write a successful book named *See Here, Private Hargrove* when you could commercialize your experiences *For Crying Out Loud, Private Wilmer,* (subtitle *I and the Armed Services.*) The trouble is no one would believe what you wrote. That is, no one except grizzled veterans of 1918 who had the bad luck to be "casuals" in that war. I have seen men who went through the worst of the Argonne, recite their experiences without turning a hair, but they showed all signs of shellshock when they recounted what happened to them when they were unassigned and "casuals." It does seem to me that a man who has worked as hard to get into the Army as you have worked should find his right slot. I hope so much you finally swing the assignment at Montgomery. Of course Montgomery has its drawbacks, in that it is almost impossible to reach any other town in the South from Montgomery unless you are willing to walk or to ride a snail. But I know you wouldn't mind that if you were near home and had a real assignment.

I am going to the *Constitution* today and if I see Ralph McGill * I'll ask him for news about you and will write you about it.

Clifford Tritchler is back home on the first leave in six months. He is an ensign in charge of a Navy gun crew in the Merchant Marine and has been all over the world since I last saw him. I ran into him at the Driving Club Saturday, waiting for the wife he married just before he went away. She was coming up from some small town and was six hours late. He'd been away so long he didn't know about the rigors of civilian travel and didn't realize that six hours late now-days is practically on time.

Sam Tupper got home the other day from Camp Crowder, having been discharged from the Army because of his "advanced age." He is in a defense plant at Cartersville. By the way the Man Power people are talking, everybody in Georgia is going to be in a defense plant before long. Hervey Allen (*Anthony Adverse*) is one of the Man Powers for this section and he says that when the Bell Bomber Plant is going full blast, next month, thirty thousand women will have to get out of Atlanta kitchens and into the assembly lines.

I'm so glad Adgate Hill is there to give you a touch of home. She is one of the nicest people I know and so is her husband. She really knows what Southern hospitality is like. Give them my best when you see them.

Just now half the town is flat on its back relaxing and breathing heavily after the windup of the two-months' "Atlanta" cruiser campaign. The goal was thirty-five million but sixty-three million was raised. There was a large to-do at the Auditorium, with Secretary Knox as the top speaker and sloughs of admirals, slathers of gold braid, so many flashlights we were blind for hours, and lots of flags. Captain Jenkins, of the "Atlanta," was here and Carl Garver, surgeon of the "Atlanta," so it was a highly successful affair emotionally as well as financially.

I am hoping your next letter will be dated Montgomery.

Good luck to you from both of us,

Peggy

* Ralph McGill was a columnist and later became the editor of the Atlanta *Constitution*.

Atlanta, Georgia

April 6, 1943

Dear Mr. Wilmer:

Mrs. Marsh wants me to thank you for your last letter and the snapshot you enclosed. They were forwarded to her at Johns Hopkins Hospital where she had gone for an operation on her back. Mr. Marsh, who went with her, is back now and he has asked me to write you about her.

Although her back has been a bother for a long time, it has not kept her from being extremely active, as you know. She was operated upon on Friday, March 26th, and she has made surprising progress. Mr. Marsh said the first two days were pretty bad and I am sure she is not without discomfort even now, but after the second night they dispensed with the special nurses and on Sunday, the following day, she was able to be propped up some in bed and to turn a little. Mr. Marsh said that almost from the beginning she looked remarkably unlike a person who had been through an operation. Her reactions were so favorable that before the week was up Mr. Marsh went over to Wilmington, Delaware, for a day or two with his mother. He stopped in Baltimore again on Friday for the day and left that night for Atlanta. A note written by Mrs. Marsh yesterday (though the writing I saw on the envelope looked like laborious bed-writing) said she had been up briefly in a chair three times since Mr. Mrash left. She is to stay on for two or three weeks, when Mr. Marsh will go back for her. After that the plan is that she will stay home quietly until she is able to go about her shipbuilding and other usual pastimes.

I know that she enjoys your letters and you may be assured that when you have time to write her again it will be forwarded.

Sincerely,

Margaret Baugh

Secretary to Mrs. Marsh

Atlanta, Georgia

May 11, 1943

Dear Cary:

My secretary, Miss Margaret Baugh, probably wrote you that I
had gone to Johns Hopkins in Baltimore for an operation. I've been
back going on three weeks. While I can walk about the apartment
half a day, laced up in a brace which makes the upper part of my
anatomy look like Mae West (John * says Air Marshal Goering), I
still haven't gotten downstairs yet.

While I was at Johns Hopkins I had a "No Visitors" sign on my
door, for I was having a pretty bad time and I did not care for casual
strangers who came in to ask for my autograph and if Clark Gable
really was darling. But one very old friend in Washington, a neo-
confederate who writes non-fiction historical books, did come to see
me. He looked at me as I lay on my bed of pain and made this
diagnosis, "What you need is a mint julep. There is a bar across the
street which probably makes mint julep with a gin base and adds
thereto a dreadful mint syrup out of a bottle and garnishes it with
chopped apples and mayonnaise. But I, who am writing a history of
General Nathan Bedford Forrest, will descend upon this bar,
decimate these Marylanders who think they are Southerners, and
mix you a julep personally. I will then hide it under the back of my
coat neatly wrapped in a napkin, and all will be well with you." I told
this eminent historian and humanitarian that I appreciated his
thought but I would wait till I got home and would ask my secretary to
step across to the Club and have Will ** shake me up a planter's
punch.

I came home on a stretcher and Miss Baugh, my secretary,
consulted with Will and brought back a brimming beaker which
made me feel much better. I thought then that my convalescence
would be a happy occasion, but, alas, have you heard the news? The
day after I got home, the Christian element in our hometown
moved in with foot and horse and tank and plane upon the clubs,
hotels, driveins, hamburger stands, houses of prostitution and soda
fountains. They invoked the law. Of course everybody had
forgotten that Georgia had a liquor store law and no mixed drinks

were supposed to be sold in the state. So no one can buy a drink at a club or a hotel or drink it in view of the public. The crusaders have fixed it so that you must go home and pull down the shades, for anyone who drinks where anyone can see them can be arrested. So that one drink I got from the Driving Club which boosted my sagging spirits after a rough ride home from Baltimore was the last mixed drink I had.

You as an old PDC member will be interested in this, I am sure. I haven't yet recovered enough to go downstairs and across the street for dinner at the Club, but John tells me that the Club is observing not only the law but the letter of the law. Beer is served and that is all. Will, the bartender, is now waiting on tables, and what it is doing to his soul I cannot say. In a way I do not blame the Christian and the godly too much, for I have heard the following: You know what a big on weekends. Like every large camp town, we have our problem of on week-ends. Like every large camp town, we have our problem of fourteen-year-old girls who are uniform-crazy. It has been very serious and the drunkenness among the young and the delinquency of those children under sixteen has been very high. No place selling liquor is supposed to sell it to minors. But the godly made test cases. They sent fourteen and fifteen-year-old children to hotels and bars and got them to order hard liquor. The children got it in any amount that they had money to pay for. Then the godly moved in on the Mayor, who closed down everything except the liquor stores. I do not care for prohibition and I am against it but I think the hotels et cetera were seriously at fault in abusing the law.

So here the town is practically where it was in 1925---you can buy liquor but you must drink it at home with the shades pulled down. The result has been that, with fury and indignation, a majority of our best-thought-of citizens have been buying liquor and drinking it with the shades pulled down and then rushing out into the streets yelling, "Hooray for hell, the devil is dead." My, my, it takes me back to the days of my youth. I am just wondering when some brash sergeant will call to see me, with corn whiskey in a Mason jar or a hot water bottle from which he has lost the stopper.

As I haven't been out of the house, I haven't much news to send you. I get a little better as the weeks go by and I hope that eventually I'll be better than I have been in many years. I've had this trouble with my back and foot since 1935 and it has been annoying and at times a severe handicap. I'm sure you'll understand the reasons why I was willing to go into this radical and serious operation. You have had a serious handicap with your leg and you have fought, bled and died to get into the service and to stay there. I fought, bled and died to do my share on Red Cross, civilian defense and bond sales. But I think we are in for a long war and the time may come when women like me who have no children will be called on to do many jobs they never expected to do. I want to be ready for any job I can fill — in the near future or in the post-war world which will be a tough but interesting world. So, I'm sitting around waiting to see how this operation on my spine will work out, and waiting with as much patience as possible, for a complete recovery. Good God, if all the colored folks I know are out sand-blasting and welding and packing parachutes, I ought to be able to do something more than the gentle business of selling bonds and making surgical dressings.

The last I heard from you was quite a while ago. I am wondering if Helena Callaway's husband swung anything your way. I certainly hope so. You've been in the service almost long enough to have a leave, and if you do come home let us know and I will have John and you (and Julius if necessary) tote me across the street so that we can sit around and have dinner and we can hear your news.

Best to you from us both,

Peggy

* John Marsh was Peggy's husband.

** Will was the bartender at the Driving Club.

Atlanta, Georgia

July 29, 1943

Dear Cary:

I am sending you Ralph McGill's column which mentions gliders. He broadcast from London the day Mussolini was deposed, telling what soldiers and civilians on the streets of London thought about the matter. I expect that, with real invasion more than a possibility now, Ralph will remain overseas longer than he expected.

I do not know if you knew Charlie Reid but I am sending you the clipping about his resignation from the supreme court. It is not stated in the story what he will do in the Army, but it is a wide open secret. He is going to one of those military schools where men are trained for administrative positions in conquered or liberated territories. I don't know if I would want a job like that. If I were a soldier I'd want to come home as soon as the war was over. In an administrative position a man might have to stay abroad until reconstruction was completed. In other words, the duration would be just the beginning.

Doctor Dan Elkin and his wife were back home on a short furlough last week. He's a colonel in the Medical Corps now and stationed at White Sulphur. Both of them looked as if the Army was agreeing with them. Jack Hickey is out of the Army and working at the Bell Bomber Plant now. I haven't seen him since he came home but those who have say he has some stories about Army life that are lulus.

I haven't any news to report, as I am still not getting out very much. I'm doing better, however, and can get along without a brace for longer intervals. In this weather that's a blessing.

John and I send our best,

Peggy

Atlanta, Georgia
August 23, 1943

Dear Cary:

I thought the enclosed clipping about the new managing editor would interest you. I do not know what has happened to Mr. Noble.

Ralph McGill is safely home but I haven't seen him yet. Naturally he is very busy and, on top of his work, he's having to see or write to the families of all the soldiers he met in England — some of whom are now missing.

I am so sorry that things are not working out too well between you and the Army and I can understand your feeling that as you are not being used to your fullest capacity you might be of more service on the outside. In case you are interested, Jack Hickey is out of the Army and at the Bell Bomber Plant. I have seen him only once, at a crowded Sunday morning party where I had little opportunity to talk to him. I think I'm right in saying that he is doing public relations there and helping get out the house paper. It might be that he could give you information.

The Air Force Show sounds fine and I hope it works out for you. I did not hear you do "The Treasurer's Report" but heard how fine you were in it. It's one of my favorite recitations.

We've just been through a trying week, due to a broadcast by one Jimmie Fidler. He went on the air at the top of his voice Sunday-before-last, announcing that I was "under the care of a Chicago specialist." Within twelve hours everybody had me blind, in Chicago, having an operation in a Chicago hospital, et cetera. I can't imagine how it all started, for I'm having no eye trouble and have never been in Chicago. It's been a mess of answering telephone calls and wiring Fidler for a correction and having the AP carry the right story, et cetera. Filder corrected it last night, but so briefly and so fast that he sounded as if he were gargling. The irresponsibles on newspaper columns and on the air have caused me more trouble than autograph hunters, and that is saying a lot.

I see by the papers your people are here and I'm going to try to see them.

Best to you,

Peggy

Atlanta, Georgia

October 7, 1943

Dear Cary:

Yes, I sent you the Heinz * clipping. This murder has had Atlanta by the ear, as you can well imagine, and I do not recall anything in years which has so genuinely shocked people. The feeling was many times worse than when the Negro burglar shot Doctor Hines Roberts's wife, Delia Johnston, for she was not killed. So far, there is not a clue to the whole affair. In the absence of truth, the most remarkable rumors have risen, some of them so incredible that I cannot understand how even morons would repeat them. Every day the papers come out denying another rumor. Mr. Heinz was a fine person and always up to some good work for Atlanta. There are a lot of people who could have been shot and the town been far less regretful.

It was fun seeing Claude and I know he must have told you that he and Ann and I had a fine though brief session. He told me just a little about your problems and about your chance at the bomber plant. As we were at the PDC and people were charging up and saying hello, I did not ask him too many questions, as I thought you probably did not want your business bruited about too much.

I believe I told you long ago that Sam Tupper had been discharged from the Army when he reached the advanced age of thirty-eight, and he is now in public relations, getting out the house organ et cetera, at the Atco plant in Cartersville. As his family lives outside of Cartersville now, it is very convenient all the way round. I have no idea through what channels his discharge came or how he was allotted to Atco. I understand he had a choice between Atco and the LaGrange Mills. I know Sam would be happy to give you any informaton he had if you would write him. The address is Samuel Y. Tupper, Junior, Birdwood, Cartersville, Georgia.

Your idea about getting back into the Army again from civilian life and making a try for a commission in the Military Government setup sounds good. It sounds queer, however, that a man would have a better chance to do something like this if he came direct from civilian life — but, after all, this is the second war I have seen and I know a little about the Army and nothing surprises me. I do not recall if I sent you clippings about Chief Justice Charles Reid resigning from the bench and going into the Military Government School. I haven't an idea where he is or what has happened to him. Did you know him? If you do, he might be a lead to follow. He is the only person I've heard of from Atlanta who has gone into this branch, though there may be others who were less well known and drew lower commissions. Mr. Reid drew a lieutenant colonelcy. I have a friend in Washington who is in a desperately essential war job and who almost found himself on his way to North Africa as a part of the Military Government. During the last war he had been the boss of several towns in Germany during the occupation. His company went into catfits and wouldn't let him go. It might be that he could cast some light on how one goes about such things, and when and if you get your furlough, remind me to discuss him with you if you are interested.

Did you know Wright Bryan ** was in England? I didn't know he was going and did not see him before he left but I'd heard that the *Journal* had been dancing up and down with impatience ever since Ralph McGill went abroad. He has sent back four or five shorts from England, most of them being concerned with Atlanta and Georgia people he has met there. Things are comparatively dull in England now and all there is to write about is the fortress raids, and everybody has taken a whack at them. If he manages to stay over until the Continent is invaded, the *Journal* will certainly be snooting the *Constitution* at having him there while Ralph is home again. From a physical point of view, I can't think of two worse correspondents. Mary Elizabeth McGill said she hated to think of Ralph in a landing barge on a Norwegian beach because he would present so large a target that no German could miss him. Wright is so tall that no foxhole would hold all of him and he would be a pretty target in a landing barge, too, unless he sat down all the time.

It would be wonderful if you got a Christmas furlough or if you got your discharge around Christmas. I know how much it would mean to your people to have you for the holidays — and I know what it would mean to you, too. Keep us posted about what happens along these lines.

Tell Claude Herndon that I incautiously told his story about the lady who couldn't get the proper evening dress at Bonwit-Teller's to Mary Ballenger Foster, who is in the hospital recovering from an operation. The effect was fine and the joke went over well but it almost wrecked both of us. This joke involves a multiplicity of spinal movements which I hadn't made since my operation. And Mary laughed so loudly she pulled a stitch.

John sends his best along with mine,

Peggy

* Henry Heinz was the husband of Lucy Candler, the only daughter of Coca-Cola founder Asa G. Candler.

** Wright Bryan

Atlanta, Georgia

December 10, 1943

Dear Cary:

If you come home Christmas, don't forget to call us up because we'd like to buy you a drink and hear all your news. If you don't come home, we'll be thinking about you and hoping you are having a good time at Adgate's. Do let us know how things have worked out about your possible discharge. There's no particular news — that is, none that I know of personally. I do not circulate much these days, and so I do not pick up much gossip.

All good wishes to you from us both,

Peggy

Atlanta, Georgia

May 8, 1944

Dear Cary;

I have been awful about writing you. I've laid off a dozen times to
do it and each time something happens which keeps me running for
a week or so. I intended writing you immediately after my brief time
with Claud but, as you see, I did not manage it. I didn't know Claud
was coming and nearly fell over when he rushed out of the Driving
Club and embraced me as I was prancing down Piedmont Avenue.
He was waiting to have lunch with Adgate and Ewell and was on his
way up to our apartment. I bought him a drink and ate a quick
sandwich with him, and Adgate and Ewell and we made plans to
have lunch the next day. I invited Ann Couper to be with us. It's
lucky I did, for the next morning I was as sick as I have ever been in
my life. I took a dose of a new cough medicine, and if it had been
ipecac I could not have fared worse. As time went on and I knew I
could not make the lunch date, I phoned Ann and told her to take
care of Claud, as I could not be with them. Evidently she took care
of him in a big way, for she phoned me around five o'clock, drooling
and smacking her chops. She said she knew she'd never have the
opportunity again so she had thrown the thirty-five-cent blue plate
special out of the window and she and Claud had lunched lavishly
on champagne cocktails and lobster thermidor. Ann had signed
John's name to the bill. We haven't yet had the courage to ask Mr.
Edwards how much the bill was.

So you see I really did not get any opportunity to talk to Claud.
When I first saw him he told me that you had sent your regards and
that you were living downtown instead of at the Barracks. Yes, he
said you had something to do with the WAC recruiting campaign
and I thought that very fine indeed. Heaven knows the need for
additional WACs is great and evidently it's going to take smart
work to get recruits. If you are handling press releases or anything
connected with the WAC you are doing a swell job. The main thing
is that you are happy and you like your work. As I told you before,
I've always respected you a lot because of your struggles to get into
the Army when others were trying to get out, and your present

struggles to stay in the Army, in spite of the "permanently disqualified" rating given by the medicos, when others are trying to get out of the Army.

I hope so much you manage to get your short vacation this month. I'll keep my ear cocked for a phone call around the 17th. Perhaps by that time it will be hot enough for John and me to buy you a mint julep. I know you won't believe it, but yesterday there was frost in low places. We've had the coldest, wettest spring in nearly fifty years. The very idea of a frosted julep brings on goosepimples. It's more like Tom and Jerry weather.

I've seen Adgate several times but mainly in large parties and hardly got a chance to talk to her. I'm hoping to have her for lunch alone sometime soon. Father's illness, coupled with illness among his orderlies, has kept me from much social life recently.

If you don't get home this month, write and tell me how you are doing in the Public Relations. If you are coming home, save all your news and we will have a big gabfest.

Affectionately,

Peggy

Atlanta, Georgia

September 12, 1944

Dear Cary:

I was suprised to hear from you in Chicago. Your new setup sounds even better than the one you left behind you, but I know you must have been sorry to leave the friends you made in Saint Louis, and especially Adgate and Walter Hill's private USO. Being only a country girl and hardly ever out of Fulton County, my notions of distances in the West are very vague and I have no idea if Saint Louis is close enough to Chicago for you to get there on weekends. Perhaps you won't miss Saint Louis too much, for, from all I have

heard of Chicago, it is one of the most exciting cities in the United
States. It is true most of my information has been gathered from
memoirs of newspapermen who worked there between 1914 and
the repeal of prohibition. Perhaps it isn't quite as colorful now. No, I
do not think Sitting Bull and his warriors are on the outskirts of the
town ready to scalp the settlers, nor do I think private wars are going
on merrily in Cicero. I realize, sadly, that newspapers are not
conducted along the lines of "Front Page." But, even with all these
enchanting inducements taken away, Chicago remains a very
vigorous place and I hope you enjoy it.

All the foregoing leads up to your remark about the post-war
possibilities of Chicago and the opportunities there. It would be
wonderful if you could land a fine job there and have it waiting for
you when you are demobilized. I think you are very smart to be
thinking about your post-war plans, for victory on the European
front, at least, seems rapidly approaching. Of course that does not
mean that the Army will turn everybody loose, for God only knows
how long the war in the Pacific will go on. Still, it's good business to
be looking around.

I was at the *Constitution* recently and ran into Lee Furman. * He
said he had a motion he wanted me to bring up at the next meeting
of the Atlanta Women's Press Club. It was that he thought the Press
Club ought to invite the male members of the *Constitution* staff as
their guests at their next party. When I mentioned this to some of
the *Constitution* girls and said how could our treasury be stretched to
cover so many guests, they laughed heartily — "Lee Furman is almost
the only male left on the staff." It is the same on the *Journal.* The City
Room looks like a young ladies' finishing school. Mr. Kirkpatrick **
and Fred Moon *** report that the girls do excellent work and that
they are pleased with them. Still, it does seem strange to me to see
childish looking young ladies with flowers in their pompadours
covering beats that were from the beginning of newspapers the
exclusive possessions of men.

You know Rosalie Davis who married Mart Bailey, don't you? I
just read in the morning paper that the War Department had
reported Mart, Jr. killed in action in France. He married Cason
Callaway's daughter and they have a young son. The Davises have
been neighbors of ours on Peachtree ever since we moved there
long ago and I cannot tell you how bad I feel about this. But two

more cheerful things — did you know Venice Mason, wife of Colonel Philip Fry who was captured at Corrigador? After complete silence from him since his capture, she has recently had four prisoner-of-war letters. The latest one was only four months old. At the same time, General Ned King's wife had six letters from the General. He was taken prisoner at the same time Phil was captured. Both Venice and Mrs. King have worked so hard and loyally in the Red Cross that the happiness of those of us who have worked with them is great. I know Venice must have thought her husband was dead, but she certainly never showed her feeling to anyone.

Although Father died in June, I have still hardly made a dent on things that piled up at that time. That's the reason I haven't written you long before this. My brother and I have not even had the opportunity to go over Father's library and select the books we want, nor have we had time to go through his letters and papers. I hope so much to get caught up by the first of the year and to start off the new year even.

Lamar Trotti is in town for the Southern premiere of his picture *Wilson*. I had invitations to various public and private parties given for him, but, as I am not going out to parties yet, I know it's not likely that I'll see him. It is nice to have a home town boy make good and I hope his *Wilson* is a success. I understand that with his next picture, *Colonel Effingham's Raid*, by Berry Fleming of Augusta, Lamar becomes a full-fledged producer. I sometimes ponder on these alleged premieres and wonder what purpose it serves to have movie stars who are unconcerned with the film hauled about the country and put on exhibit. Little Roddy McDowell, who stared in *How Green Was My Valley*, is in town now and, bewilderingly enough, so is Carmen Miranda. Just what they have to do with the life of Woodrow Wilson I do not know.

John sends his best and so do I, and all good wishes for this new job.

Peggy

* Lee Furman was a reporter for the *Constitution*.

** Mr. Kirkpatrick was an editor for the *Constitution*.

*** Fred Moon was also an editor for the *Constitution*.

Yolande Gwin

Atlanta, Georgia

June 6, 1945

Dear Cary:

What on earth! I never heard of anything as mysterious as your illness. I am certainly glad the Medical Corps put you in the bed and I hope they've found out what is wrong. It is bad enough to be sick, but to have the cause of the sickness a mystery would make it worse.

When I had not heard from you for some time I wondered if you had gotten your discharge on account of age and gone to work in Chicago as you had tentatively planned. I had thought you so busy on a new civilian job you didn't have time to write. I am sorry my suppositions were wrong. It seems to me that if you are to be forty this fall you are eligible for a discharge. At least I read in the papers that men over thirty-five are to be let out and eighteen-year-olds inducted to take their places. Or is that just on paper?

Write and tell us if there's any particular piece of reading matter you'd like to have and we'll get it for you. That's about all a civilian can offer a soldier these days. I wish you were in a hospital closer to Atlanta and then we could come to see you. Please let us know how you get along. Do your people know about this illness? I haven't opened my mouth about it for fear someone I told might somehow get the news to your family, and I did not know if that was what you wanted. Here's hoping they let you out of the hospital soon, and here's hoping you'll be well when they do.

Peggy

MARTIN

Harold Martin, a long time columnist for The Atlanta Constitution, was a marine during the "40's" and stationed off Tokyo. He wrote the following column after the war and was back in Atlanta:
The Atlanta Constitution

August 11,1947.

SOME MEMORIES OF PEGGY

I remember one night off Tokyo, when we had come alongside a Jap submarine, lying in the sea with her engines dead, and had taken her over to sail in as a prize of war. I went down the ladder and into the crew's quarters, looking around to see how these strange little men of an enemy race lived, and there in the dim steel room, at the foot of a bunk, still open where the reader had laid it down, was a thick book. I picked it up, greasy and torn and stained by a thousand yellow hands, and looked at it. It was in English, and it lay open at the page where Scarlett and Rhett, and that little Negro girl, were fleeing with the wagon and the spavined horse, through the ruins of burning Atlanta.

And I stood there, in a ship that travels beneath the sea, and thought of home, and Peggy Mitchell, and Gone With The Wind, **the book that swept the world. And I carried it with me the next morning as through the mists of dawn the white crown of Fujiyama glittered in the sun above a strange and alien land. And I carried it with me a long time after that, hoping to bring it back to Peggy, as a sort of souvenir until somehow, with all the shifting and the traveling, it was lost.**

The other night, in a shabby little hotel in a shabby little town in Tennessee, I picked up a paper and saw her picture, there on the front page, and the big black headline saying that she was dead. And a hundred memories came back to me of one of the finest, sweetest, persons I ever knew. I remember her before she wrote the book, and afterward, and she was always the just the same. There was nothing of the poseur about her, nothing phonily literary. She had a great tale to tell and she told it magnificently, and that was all there was. She didn't hit the glittering trail that so many writers follow to their own destruction — the literary teas, the queening it over a circle of fawning sycophants, the knifesharp criticisms of fellow authors and their works. She merely went back to being John Marsh's wife, the role she loved better than all the adulation that authorship earned her.

She was a gay, and witty, and sweet, and simple person. I remember the old parties at Nancy and Dudley Glass' house, in the Christmas holidays, with Peggy always sitting at the same spot on the stair, telling stories, and in the cool of the evening, singing a little with the gang. We didn't think of her as the star-crowned author of a best selling novel, but as one of us, as Peggy, a good reporter, relaxing a little when the time had come to relax.

She was, for all her friendliness, and for all the fame the book brought her, a shy and unpretentious person. I remember the story a neighbor of mine told. She had advertised her apartment for rent, and among the people who came to see it, was one couple who had charmed her. He was big and gentle and kind of awkward, and she was a tiny twinkle-eyed lady, and my neighbor liked them so well she thought she would like to do something for them. So, she said, she told them that if they liked the apartment, she would leave up the set of beautiful new drapes she had only recently hung, instead of taking them down and selling them as she had planned. So they thanked her warmly, and said they would think it over, and she didn't know until she asked their names again as they left, that she had been making her kindly gesture to the famous author of *Gone With The Wind*.

I remember too, the night of the premiere, when the whole town was crazy and the lights were blazing down and the glittering stars from Hollywood were causing the public to swoon. Peggy came in, composed as a tiny queen, pleased, of course, that her home folks liked the book she had written and the picture that had been made from it, but still as calm and poised as if she were merely another spectator come to see the show. Outside the theater I caught John Marsh for a moment and asked him a question or two — hunting for something that could go in the story about the premiere I was doing for the paper. He didn't even have much to say. So I told him thanks, and as he turned to go, I said:

"I guess you are pretty proud of Peggy tonight."
And he turned and stopped and laid his hand on my arm, and said:
"I was proud of Peggy before she ever wrote a book."

So I put that in the story, just as he said it, and afterward Peggy wrote me a little note, saying that of all the thousands of words that were written about the premiere, and of all the praise of the critics for her book, the line that touched her deepest and pleased her most was John's simple statement that night as he walked into the theater before the show.

And all of us who knew her understood how he felt. For we would have loved and respected her for the wonderful person she was, if she had never written a line.

The news of her passing has been told in many nations, in many languages now. And around the world folk whose hearts she touched through her novel, are calling upon whatever God they believe in, to bless and keep her on her journey.

Harold Martin sent me the following some years later. — Yolande Gwin.

Yolande: Did you ever see Margaret Mitchell make like she had a good mouthful of snuff? She could pooch out her lower lip with her tongue, and the effect was both accurate and hilarious. She would only do it in the company of her friends — I remember one night during the Georgia Press Ass'n meetings in Athens, and we were all in somebody's room in the hotel, most of us on the bed, and she did it at the behest of Walter Paschall and others. Among those present, if memory serves me correctly, were Edna Cain Daniel (Quitman, Georgia, *Free Press*, one of Peggy's *closest* friends, but I'm sure she must be gone by this time); maybe Virginia Polhill Price (The *News and Farmer*, Louisville, Georgia), and other editor/owners of Georgia newspapers, Emily Woodward, John Paschall, and that dear old chap from South Georgia, Jack — (can't recall his last name) who wore the flowing black neckties.

Memories, memories. But I thought you might relish the snuff bit, whether or not you can use it.

Best,
Martin

Harold Martin.

MADDOX

Sims Maddox, Margaret Mitchell's cousin, received the following letter from her in late 1948:

Atlanta 5 - December 1, 1948

Dear Sims:

Thank you so much for your fine letter. I would have answered it before now but I have been sick. Thank you for offering to show John and me your bullet mold. We will be very glad to see it.

Do you recall that I spoke to you about Doctor Mac West, who is now in the Army at Augusta but who returns home to visit his parents once a month? He is the one who has a number of old pistols and guns, some confederate, and he is an authority on old firearms. He will be home this weekend and he wants you and me to come to see him at the house of his father and mother, Doctor and Mrs. C.M. West, 1659 Pelham Road, N.E. He wants you to bring your pistol and gun for him to look at and he will show you his guns. Would you like to go? If you do want to go, I can come by your house for you in the automobile, at 3:30 this coming Saturday, December 4th, take you to the Wests and bring you home again. Telephone me here at home, at Hemlock 7335, as soon as you get this letter and let me know whether you want to go to see the Wests or not. I will get the pistol my grandfather carried during the time of his service in the Confederacy and which he was wearing when he was badly wounded in the Battle of Sharpsburg, and will take it with us to ask Doctor West about it. After you decide whether you want to go, I will call your Aunt Wesley and ask her to go with us.

Your cousin,

Peggy

P.S. If you do go, don't forget to bring the bullet mold. I want to see it.

ABRAMS

Dan Abrams, book dealer and publisher, says he met Margaret Mitchell through his aunt, the late Medora Field Perkerson.

After that, on my many trips to the Atlanta Public Library, I would also see Miss Mitchell researching on some subject.

I was a kid at the time and I was always interested in reading all types of books.

I always enjoyed being with Medora and Miss Mitchell. She, Margaret, was always telling interesting stories and would chat and always asked me questions as if we were the same age.

Also, I always looked forward to seeing her and talking with her as she was the most fantastic person I had ever known. I also felt close to her as she and Medora were such good friends.

One day, the three of us went to lunch at Mary Mac's restaurant on Ponce de Leon Avenue. Which we all loved. It was such a fine day and Miss Mitchell was in high spirits.

We left together, but, were in two separate cars. Miss Mitchell was with Medora and as they began to leave she told me "I'll see you again soon, I hope" and as the car rolled out she threw me a kiss!

The next evening she was hurt in that fatal crash. I'll never, never forget her.

Margaret and Medora Field Perkerson.

BRYAN

Mrs. Wright Bryan, an Atlanta native, now lives in Clemson, S.C. where her husband is president of Clemson College.

Mrs. Bryan, the former Ellen Newell, has many happy memories of Peggy Mitchell, although the latter was a bit older than Mrs. Bryan they both attended Washington Seminary, a private school in Atlanta.

Wright and I were dinner one night at the Piedmont Driving Club. Wright was then editor of the Atlanta *Journal*. He received a call about Peggy's accident.

Then we went to Grady Hospital where she had been taken.

I returned to the hospital every day to help man the phones on the first floor. Calls came from all over the country and the world.

As you know, John Marsh, (her husband) was a very sick man even then. And no one was allowed in Peggy's room.

Many people came to the hospital hoping to call on Peggy and many friends of Peggy's were there to halt any invasion.

Reporters from over the nation were also there. To our horror one reporter, from out of town, was told he couldn't see her. "Oh yes I will," he shouted, and left the lobby. Later, he reappeared wearing hospital attire, went to her room, passed himself as an intern and walked right on in.

Her brain damage was too severe to operate on her or even move her to another room.

Her funeral was by invitation only.

I'll miss her the rest of my life.

Admit Bearer

to services for

Mrs. John R. Marsh

Thursday, August eighteenth, 1949

at ten o'clock, A.M.

Spring Hill

HEALEY

Mrs. William Healey, the former Callie Orme, had the following to say:

I did not know Peggy as well as did my sister Sarah (Mrs. William Huger). However, when Ellen and Wright (Mr. and Mrs. Wright Bryan) would have small groups at their home so very often Peggy was there and of course entertained all of us with her usual and witty conversation.

Whenever the Bryan's had her at their home they would provide her with a small footstool for her to put her feet on as she was so tiny. The Bryans had mostly large chairs but Peggy with her footstool could be cozy as all of us.

All of us, including Peggy would sit around and sip bourbon. Those were happy days. How she ever wrote that big book will always be a mystery to me.

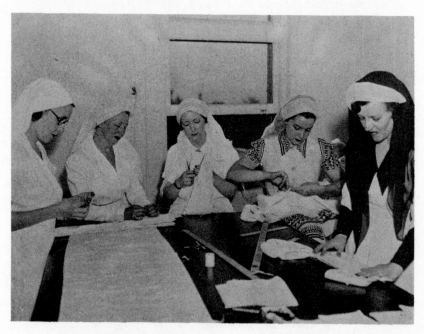

Margaret rolling bandages at the Red Cross.

SHARP

Mrs. Marguerite Sharp, the former Marguerite Scott, of Atlanta was first married to Glascock Reynolds, brother of Mrs. Stephens Mitchell.

When Peggy was injured and was taken to Grady Hospital, Mrs. Stephens Mitchell asked me to go to the hospital in her place as she was, at the time, ill in bed. I went right to the hospital and stood outside Peggy's room to keep an inquiring public away. One reporter kept trying to go into Peggy's room and see that she was given some aspirin. He claimed aspirin would cure everything. I finally got rid of him.

And another reporter kept hanging around as he had heard Peggy had all of her hair shaved off. I finally told him to take a picture of the door to her room as it had her name on it. He thought that was a good idea. So he took the picture and left.

When Peggy died, Mrs. Stephens Mitchell asked me to tell Mr. Marsh that it would be a good idea to send out cards for the funeral. "If not" she added, "There would be a mob scene at the service." John Marsh took her advice and had the cards mailed. (In the old days cards were hand delivered.)

The service was held at Patterson's Funeral Home in Atlanta. The place was packed and hundreds were outside along Spring Street. Dean Raimundo de Ovies of the Atlanta Episcopal Diocese officiated. The burial was in the Mitchell lot at Oakland Cemetery where so many of the Confederate dead are buried.

GERAKITIS

Mrs. George Gerakitis, the former Mynita Swan, lives in Northwest Atlanta, was at one time a fashion columnist for the Atlanta Constitution *prior to its merger with the* Atlanta Journal. *Her byline was Mynita Gerry.*

In 1951, a day or so after June 13, which was the day on which Charles, son number two, was born. Mother was visiting me at St. Joesph's Infirmary, but, only ostensibly . . . . she was really there to make time with her newest grandson. Anyway, during Mother's visit, Sister Melanie, the nun who had been in the delivery room when Charlie was born, came in. I introduced her to Mother, of course, whereupon Mother asked her if she had taken her name Melanie from a sister Melanie, who had taught her (Mother) in Augusta, quite a few years back.

Sister Melanie said something to the effect that both she and the Melanie in *Gone With The Wind* shared that special distinction. It seems, according to the story Sister Melanie then told Mother and me, that the original Sister Melanie (the one who had taught Mother) was a relative of Peggy Mitchell's, a very special one whom Peggy admired very much, whose character was the one after which she patterned the Melanie in her book. Feeling perhaps that it would please Sister Melanie that she had given her name to the most exemplary character in her book, Peggy gave her one of the first editions of her book.

After reading the book, Sister Melanie, was hardly pleased. She was apoplectic. She was fit to be tied. She was one furious lady of the cloth.

Her critique was short and straight to the point:

"Margaret," she demanded, "take me out of that terrible book!"

Photo Section

Post-Book
Era

Associated Press photo of Margaret receiving an Honorary Degree from Smith College chatting with Elizabeth M. Neilson.

Margaret and Florence Miles of The *Journal* copy desk with their prize-winning entries in The Magazine's Second Annual All-Fools' Art Show.

Margaret Slices Atlanta's 100th birthday cake.

Margaret with James Cox, owner of Cox Newspapers.

Margaret and Bessie Jordan preparing relief packages for post-war Europe.

The last picture of Margaret taken by Cone Maddox in the summer of 1949.

Permanent exhibit in the lobby of the *Journal-Constitution* Building.

Worth Repeating. . .

The following articles, arranged in chronological order, are reprinted with permission from other sources.

The Atlanta *Journal*
Monday, August 26, 1974

GONE WITH THE WIND REUNION PARTY

By Yolande Gwin

Remember in the book and in the movie of *Gone With The Wind*, Scarlett O'Hara had the green velvet draperies in the parlor at Tara taken down to make a dress for her to wear to Atlanta to see Rhett Butler?

And Rhett had been jailed by the Yankees. Remember?

Well, keep on remembering, but keep this in the back of your head. In the MGM movie version of this great book by Atlanta's Margaret Mitchell, the dress was made first and then the draperies, even to the tassel tiebacks, were made.

Walter Plunkett, one of Hollywood's foremost designers, flew here for the weekend to attend a reunion luncheon given by MGM at the Diplomat, which gathered a handful of the news media who were covering at the world premiere here in 1939. He designed every costume Scarlett wore in the movie. The luncheon was a forerunner of the current showing of the Oscar winning movie now here.

"The major point in the drapery dress made it a real challenge," said the award winning Plunkett before the luncheon. "It, of all costumes had to be completely right. Because of this, they (MGM) permitted me to design the outfit first, then they made the draperies to correspond. In other words, the drapes had to be equipped with the proper tie-back cords and tassels to form the trim of the dress."

"Strangely enough, few people noticed the hat. If you look closely, you'll see it was trimmed with chicken feathers and gilded chicken feet."

According to the designer, *Gone With The Wind* posed many an unusual problem for those concerned with the costuming.

"Take Scarlett's first wedding dress for example," he said. "This was a hasty wartime marriage. Scarlett's dress was the one that had been worn by her mother. To get the authentic 'taken in' look, we actually made the dress on the dressmaker's form of Barbara O'Neil, who played her mother in the film. The design was also 20 years before the date of the story."

Mr. Plunkett is a quiet, tall, distinguished looking man who has now retired, but started out in Hollywood years ago. He has dressed the world's most beautiful women and has a designing influence on the lives of such women as Katherine Hepburn, Ava Gardener, Elizabeth Taylor, Lana Turner, Shirley MacLaine, Judy Garland and Vivien Leigh to name a few. His designs for *Gone With The Wind* helped make it a masterpiece.

"I read the book twice," he told Stephens Mitchell, brother of the author, at the luncheon. "The first time was for pleasure. The second time with pencil in hand I made notations of every line and passage containing a reference to clothes or related subjects. Your sister was one of the most charming women I've ever met and she was a great help in introducing me to people working in museums in Charleston, Savannah and here."

Mr. Plunkett has been back to Atlanta only one time since the trip when he worked with Miss Mitchell on the dress designs.

"I came back to the second premiere," he recalled. "I remember going out to a party after the show at the home of Mr. and Mrs. Kennedy (Alfred). Your First Lady of Georgia was there, and she looked lovely and was wearing one of the gowns I designed for Elizabeth Taylor to wear in *Raintree County*." As I recall, the picture here then was for a centennial celebration."

(The First Lady referred to was Mrs. Ernest Vandiver and the events were for the Centennial and Mrs. Kennedy was the chairman.)

At the reunion luncheon Secretary of State Ben Fortson was one of the honorees. Another guest was British actor Jan Hanson, who played the part of Charles Hamilton, Scarlett's first husband, in the stage version of the book in London. He is now a member of the cast of *As You Like It* which has just completed a run here. Scarlett and Rhett were there too. The two wax figures were from the wax museum Underground Atlanta.

This writer, wearing a Coca-Cola bottle opener necklace, was told this by Mr. Plunkett:

"Better hold on to that, you can make money on it. I was in an antique shop in Los Angeles recently and there was a wooded case holding 24 empty coke bottles. I know all of us have had those in days gone by, but guess what the price was? $115. Can you believe it?"

Just before rushing away from the luncheon to see the Atlanta Historical Society's exhibit at Neiman-Marcus which includes many *Gone With The Wind* items as well as one of his original costume sketches, he said:

"One more thing I must tell you about Atlanta. On my first visit here doing research I had a call from a woman who said she had saved innumerable hoops and different types of underwear and corsets. These items, believe it or not, were hard to find, even in the most complete museums.

"I finally found the house and rang the doorbell. A woman peeked through the curtains and motioned me to wait. Finally, the door opened and a little old lady, I'm sure was up in her 70's, apologized. She had had to put her mother in another room in the house and locked the door, all because I was wearing a blue suit.

Mother, it seems, thought I was a Yankee and was about to grab her rifle! (Yankee soldiers wore blue uniforms.)

So with that, Mr. Plunkett was *Gone With The Wind* himself. And he's probably back now in his beloved California. Now retired, he lives in an apartment overlooking the Pacific. He has been touring Europe in a trailer and stopping to record on canvas in oil, subjects that interest him.

Stephens Mitchell and Walter Plunkett.

The Atlanta *Journal* Thursday, June 5, 1975

JAPANESE TV FILM

GONE WITH THE WIND

SESSION

By Yolande Gwin

To update the record, Margaret Mitchell worked on The Atlanta *Journal Sunday Magazine.* (Now The Atlanta *Journal-Constitution Magazine.*)
This was before she wrote *Gone With The Wind.* In fact, her desk is still in the building.

So, the other day, Andy Sparks, editor of the magazine called and said:
"There are four visitors up here who want to know something about Margaret Mitchell. Since you knew her and wrote the first story on *Gone With The Wind*, how about coming up?" (The magazine office is on the seventh floor of the ANI building.)

A small, trim little Japanese girl with long black hair wearing a pants outfit and three men were bent over a table looking at some issues of the magazine — in bound files — which carried some of Peggy's by-lined stories.

Andy Sparks was telling them all about the stories and then showed her picture on the wall.

"Oh, here is Miss Gwin," he said and all the Japanese smiled and bowed. Then, one of them spoke in English flavored with an Oriental accent.

"We are traveling throught the United States collecting information on three of America's outstanding authors. We have been to Hannibal, Mo., where Mark Twain was born. After our stay here in Atlanta to gather material on Margaret Mitchell, we are going to Florida, well to Key West, because our third author is Ernest Hemmingway. We are told he wrote some of his famous book *The Old Man And The Sea*, there. It all sounded very interesting and thrilling especially that Atlanta's own Margaret Mitchell was one of the Big Three.

Then the Japanese visitor continued.

"We will be broadcasting three programs from Tokyo June 27, our TV station is No. 12 there. Now, will you please step into this private room (It was Andy Spark's office) so that we can set up our TV camera. While we are setting it — the camera — up, be thinking of some things about Miss Mitchell. Things like: Did she pattern Scarlett after after any members of her family? How different was Scarlett from Melanie Wilkes? Was Scarlett patterned after Miss Mitchell herself?" "Did anyone help her write the book? Did she do much research? And just any other bits of information you know. We will shoot today and again tomorrow. Now, Miss Gwin, take your glasses off. The camera lights will bounce on the glass and the picture will not be good."

By that time, the camera was turned on, and the pretty little Japanese girl sat down. One man was working the camera, the other holding the lights. The other Japanese was standing by later giving an occasional nod of approval. Andy Sparks was sitting on the other side of the Japanese girl.

"I better take my glasses off, too," Andy said. "I don't know why I am sitting here because you are the one being interviewed."

The man who had been doing all the talking said:

"All right now, you are on camera, Miss Gwin. Start the interview dear," he said to the little Japanese girl.

Well, she started all right. And her entire questioning for at least five minutes was in Japanese. She did not speak one word of English. What could one do but listen and pretend to understand?

At last, the English speaking Japanese said:

"Now Miss Gwin, don't look back here to me just keep looking at her and I will interpret her questions into English and you answer and then I will repeat your answers into Japanese to her. And don't MOVE.

This went on for about half an hour. Then the man said:

"Fine! Now wear the same outfit tomorrow for we will be back for the second part of the program."

Then he handed out his card with his name: Hiromasa Shibazaki. He is vice president of the International Research and Development Division of the T.S. Electric Corp. which has its headquarters in Tokyo.

Then there were more cards and identifications. The man who was nodding his approval at the TV filming is Tadahisa Nishi, assistant chief manager of Tokyo Channel 12 TV, Ltd., in Tokyo. The cameraman was Toshio Isofami and the pretty girl is Keiko Fujita, a well known and popular Japanese actress. None spoke English.

Shibazaki, the one who spoke English, said his company has done similar programs on such writers as Emily Bronte, Shakespeare, Hans Christian Anderson, Goethe, Tolstoy and many others. After their stay in Florida, the group was going to New Orleans.

The second day's shooting was just the same. Questions and answers in Japanese. They wanted to know, among other things, how Miss Mitchell ran her house. Was she a good housekeeper? Did she like to cook? Did she have any pets? As a little girl and later as a young college girl living on Peachtree Street, did she entertain very much and what type entertaining did she do? And many other questions.

It was a great and fun situation, but having somebody behind you answering what you said in Japanese and then asking something else in English was a little unnerving.

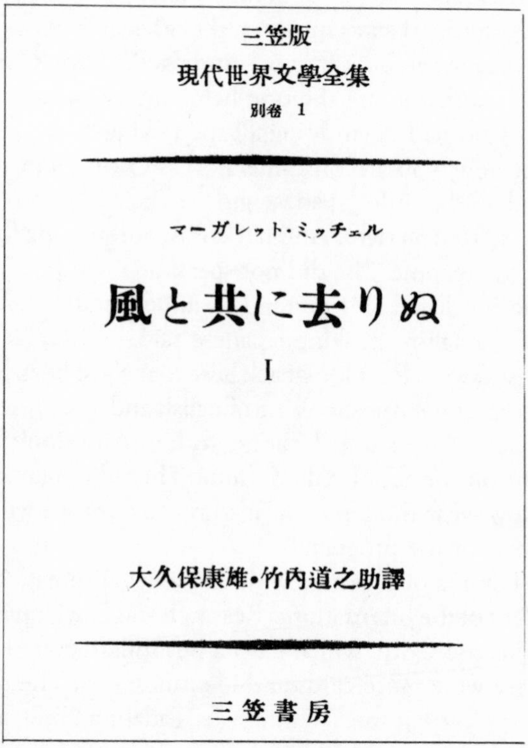

三笠版
現代世界文學全集
別巻 1

マーガレット・ミッチェル

風と共に去りぬ

I

大久保康雄・竹内道之助譯

三笠書房

Title page of a Japanese edition of *Gone With The Wind*.

Intown Extra, November 28,1985

OH, RHETT, CAN IT REALLY BE 50 YEARS?

By Yolande Gwin

Gone With The Wind madness was quite evident the other night at the Dekalb Historical Society's headquarters in Decatur at an opening night party to unveil the society's new exhibit of *Gone With The Wind* memorabilia.

Glass-top cases were filled with *Gone With The Wind* objects such as the massive collection of Herb Bridges, whose memorabilia collection is well known. Next year will mark the 50th anniversary of the publication of Margaret Mitchell's Civil War classic.

Several hundred people gathered for the showing of the exhibit. Margaret Perrin, known s the city's "society pianist," was playing popular tunes.

There seemed to be a crowd gathered all evening in one corner of the room, for there sat *Gone With The Wind* movie star, "Prissy," who had come down from her home in New York to attend. Her name, of course, is Butterfly McQueen. She sat all evening in a comfortable chair and had a great time being introduced to many guests.

She wore two corsages — one on her shoulder and one tied to her wrist. She still has that high-pitched voice that is so well remembered from the movie. As the years have passed, she has gained some weight, but is still unmistakably Prissy.

On the cover of the invitations to the party was that ever-popular picture of Rhett holding Scarlett's hands as she cried, but the caption was different. It read: "Oh, Rhett, can it really be 50 years?"

Gone With The Wind posters were hanging about the room, and many magazines with covers and stories about the 1939 premiere were displayed.

Manuel Mallof was honorary chairman of the event and honorary hosts were members of the DeKalb County Board of Commissioners. Committee members were Patsy Wiggins, Mr. and Mrs. Albert Sydney Johnson, Mr. and Mrs. Robert E. Lanier, Mr. and Mrs. Richard F. Livingston, Mr. and Mrs. Robert C. McMahon, and Mr. and Mrs. J. David Chestnut.

Dorothy Nix is Executive Director of the DeKalb Historical Society.
James W. Morton, III of Savannah designed the exhibit.

Yolande Gwin and Prissy.

Photo Section

DeKalb Historical Society Exhibit

The following pictures were taken by Franklin Nix at the DeKalb Historical Society exhibit of memorabilia of Margaret Mitchell and *Gone With The Wind*.

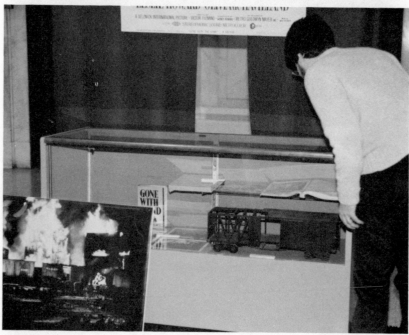

THE BIG BOOK

Reprinted with permission. Copyright © 1986, Madison-Morgan Cultural Center — Madison, Georgia.

Gone With The Wind made its author famous, an overnight celebrity in the summer of 1936 and in 1986 a figure of growing importance in the history of American literature. It made Atlanta and Georgia familiar place-names to the rest of the world. By informing readers about the American Civil War it convinced Europeans that the United States had a history of its own. If Margaret Mitchell's novel perpetuated a myth, it made lasting a region's belief in its vision of itself.

Acclaimed by reviewers but berated by more serious critics (those Margaret Mitchell described as "aesthetes and left-wingers") Gone With The Wind is literature of people. Detractors assailed it but failed to put it down. Revisionist historians pointed out flaws in its interpretations of the Civil War and of Reconstruction, but an old newspaper friend of Miss Mitchell's had the word for all that. Mildred Seydell wrote in the Atlanta Georgian of June 17, 1936 a column that was high praise of the younger woman's work. Mrs. Seydell noted that she could not vouch for GWTW's truth as official history might record it but that she could say positively that it was every inch the truth as she learned it from her own parents and grandparents, Georgians who had lived through the war years of 1861-65.

The extent of the history in Gone With The Wind is deceptive. There is little of military history. Its history is the history of the little things of life — how women made hats of cornshucks, buttons from seeds, food from wild plants (even from weeds), how they nursed wounded soldiers, and how they held up the morale of the Confederacy even past the sticking point. This homely history is the history of which Margaret Mitchell was an unmatched master.

What makes Gone With The Wind such a fine historical novel is that it does not overdo the history in it. It is first and foremost a rattling good story. Too much filling in with history has been the fatal flaw of many a novel that otherwise might have been very good, just as too much fiction introduced as fact has ruined many a so-called book of history.

On its publication date, June 30, 1936, GWTW was already an assured success. Nearly a hundred thousand copies were by then in print. Its millionth copy came off the press early in December. Distribution by the Book-of-the-Month Club in 1936 and 1937 totalled 188,000 copies, nearly three times the average rate of the book club's other selections in those years. It led the national best-seller lists in both 1936 and 1937. It has sold over five million in hardback copies, possibly as many as fifteen million in paperback. It has been translated into twenty-seven languages and its worldwide sales (including a number of pirated editions) are estimated at about thirty million.

For *Gone With The Wind* Macy's New York store once made one of the biggest book orders in publishing history — for fifty-thousand copies. That store and its rival, Gimbel's, were using it as a "loss leader" in a price war. When it was determined that Federal price controls applied to sales of *Gone With The Wind*, Macy's made the largest book return in history. Thirty-five thousand copies were trucked back to Macmillan.

The Macmillan Publishing Company claims that *GWTW* still sells daily a hundred copies in hardback and a thousand copies in paperback in the United States alone. Macmillan will publish a fiftieth anniversary edition, nominally on the anniversary of its official publication date. The Book-of-the-Month Club will offer its own anniversary edition.

The most valuable edition of *Gone With The Wind* is, logically enough, its first. Ten thousand copies of the first printing were issued, but a copy from that printing with a dust jacket in good to fine condition (particularly such a copy autographed or inscribed) is now a collector's item of considerable value. There are additional "points" that make a first printing of interest to bibliophiles, but identification of it is very easy. It has on the back of the title page the words "Published May, 1939."

Printing followed printing so fast that *GWTW*'s only textual error was not corrected until printing in August 1936. The first issue contained only two typographical errors, an amazing proof-reading achievement by the author, her husband, and Macmillan's Susan Prink. The errors were not corrected until the fourth printing of January 1937.

The rarest American edition of *GWTW* is that produced for the dedication of WSB's "White Columns on Peachtree" in April 1956. Only five hundred copies were issued. They are bound in brown skivered leather, gold stamped, and include a frontispiece showing an artist's rendering of the WSB building.

The story of Margaret Mitchell is too well known to detail here. She was born November 8, 1900, the daughter of Eugene Muse Mitchell and Maybelle Stephens Mitchell. She was educated in Atlanta's public schools and at Washington Seminary. She spent one year at Smith College. In 1919, some months after the death of her mother, she returned to Atlanta to keep house for her father and brother in a handsome home on

Peachtree, near Seventeenth Street.

In September 1922 Miss Mitchell married Berrien K. ("Red") Upshaw. The two separated after less than three months. She then got a job on the staff of the *Atlanta Journal Sunday Magazine*, where she worked until 1926. July 4, 1926 she married John Robert Marsh, publicity manager of the Georgia Power Company. For some years in the twenties she suffered from arthritis and was more or less an invalid. She wrote to amuse herself and to try to supplement the couple's income. Failing to sell any short stories (later destroyed) she began in 1927 a long novel, built with vivid imagination and a hitherto unrevealed genius for storytelling on characters she had met in family and Clayton County lore.

She made no effort to sell her novel. How she was coaxed into offering it to Harold Latham of the Macmillan Company is both history and folklore and about as well known as *Gone With The Wind* itself. She handed Latham her manuscript in April 1935. By mid-summer it had been accepted and a contract signed. She spent October 1935 through January 1936 carefully rewriting it and confirming the accuracy of its historical details. The manuscript went to the printer in February 1936. Proof was read in March. Bound copies became available in May.

Macmillan was well aware that it had a "big book." The firm devoted to it the largest advertising budget in the company's history to that time. *Gone With The Wind*'s selection by the Book-of-the-Month Club delayed its release until June 30. The extra time was well used for promotional purposes and the first printing was sold out long before publication date.

Margaret Mitchell did not take to fame. She resisted it as well as she could. It overtook her. It overwhelmed her. She became a virtual prisoner of her own fame. She autographed scores, perhaps hundreds of copies of *Gone With The Wind* before she quit autographing in December 1936. She wrote thousands of letters to readers of her novel. She spent endless hours in the direct management of the foreign publishing rights to her book and in fighting actual or contemplated infringements of her copyright.

During World War II she did Red Cross work. She sold government bonds. She worked as a neighborhood defense warden. And she christened two cruisers *Atlanta*. She was constantly helping in the care of her aging father, and, after her husband suffered a severe heart attack, she was unflagging in nursing him.

She never wrote another book. She talked of writing again, but she was a very smart woman and it is doubtful indeed that she would ever

have brought herself to compete with the success of *Gone With The Wind*.
She was fatally injured when hit by a speeding taxicab on Peachtree
Street (near Thirteenth) on the evening of August 11, 1949. She died at
Grady Hospital five days later and is buried in Oakland Cemetery.

When Sam Tupper, Jr. reviewed *Gone With The Wind* for the Atlanta
Journal June 28, 1936 he concluded:

> It is not too much to say that *Gone With The Wind* is among the
> most powerful and original novels in American literature. With its
> scope, its high emotion, and shrewed picturization, it is a book to
> own and re-read and remember forever.

He was right. He was very right.

Margaret Mitchell wrote her friend Lois Cloea of the Macmillan
Company in March 1936 agreeing to the hiring of Annie Laurie Williams
as an agent for selling the film rights to GWTW: "I don't see how it could
possible be made into a movie unless the entire book was scrapped and
Shirley Temple cast as 'Bonnie,' Mae West as 'Belle' and Step'n Fetchit as
'Uncle Peter.' "

A few months later she wrote Sidney Howard, author of the
screenplay: "When I sold the book to the Selznick Company, I made it
very plain that I would have nothing to do with the picture . . . I have no
connection with the film." She had, in fact, very much to do with it
without any official connection. She helped Kay Brown, then Selznick's
east coast representative and later an extraordinarily wonderful agent for
the Mitchell interests, set up a talent search in Atlanta. She answered
questions from Selznick International Pictures' research office. She sent
its librarian a list of books she had read as background for GWTW. She
answered questions by Howard while he was working on the screenplay.
She suggested SIP's hiring of Wilbur G. Kurtz and, later, Susan Myrick as
advisers for the film.

With Kurtz and Myrick on the sets in Hollywood and Brown in
constant touch with Selznick, Margaret Mitchell stayed very much on top
of the situation. She wrote Bishop Gerald O'Hara of Savannah: "The
book is my own creation but it has long since gotten out of my hands."
Don't believe it. She gave Selznick detailed advice on two occasions and
talked to him about problems in the filming on two others. She vetoed a
scene written by F. Scott Fitzgerald because it showed Rhett driving to
Aunt Pittypat's house in Belle Watling's carriage.

Howard did a magnificent job on the screenplay. It is of little consequence that more than a dozen other writers also worked on it. Ben Hecht did some rewriting that helped in the "construction" of the script, but his chief contribution to it is the series of titles that introduces the film and its parts. The titles serve the film well and are much loved by most fans of GWTW, but Miss Mitchell particularly disliked the lines beginning "There was a land of Cavaliers and Cotton Fields called the Old South. . ." They were contrary to her conviction that she had written a realistic novel.

Oliver H.P. Garrett, John Balderston, Jo Swerling and others wrote little for the screenplay that survives the final script. What they wrote along the way was largely wiped out by a late revision by Howard in the spring of 1939. Michael Foster has recieved almost no credit for his work and deserves considerable credit. It was his reworking of the difficult section telling the events at Tara in 1864 that survives in the film. Selznick himself devised the final scenes in a way that conveys the enigmatic ending of the novel.

After its first official showing (there had been two sneak previews) to the press in Hollywood December 12, 1939, *Film Daily* raved that GWTW was "glorious entertainment, perhaps as close to perfection in all its phases as human endeavor can attain." The paper continued:

Magnificent in its spectacle, absorbing in its drama, compelling in its romance, expertly paced, sustained in its action, finely directed, ideally cast, played with a wealth of sympathy and understanding, brilliantly photographed in Technicolor and supported by one of the most stirring musical settings the screen yet has known, such is *Gone With The Wind.*

In some way or other Selznick's impress is on every frame of the film. It is David Selznick's film. It is also Sidney Howard's film. It is Vivien Leigh's film. And Clark Gable's film. And Olivia de Havilland's. And Hattie McDaniel's. And Thomas Mitchell's, Alicia Rhett's, Ona Munson's, Butterfly McQueen's. It belongs in its enduring fame to all those people and to all those others at Selznick International Pictures who were determined to stick to the basic values of this most cinematic of novels. Because they did, *Gone With The Wind* is a great motion picture. The Big Book is also The Big Film.

March 1986   Richard Harwell

Reprinted from the Atlanta Weekly magazine of The Atlanta Journal and The Atlanta Constitution, June 22, 1986.

THE NOVEL IN REVIEW

"Atlanta Author's First Novel Is Story of War Between States" was the headline for this review in 1936.

By Yolande Gwin

Yolande Gwin, a society columnist for The Atlanta Journal *and* The Atlanta Constitution, *wrote one of the first reviews of* Gone With the Wind. *It appeared in* The Constitution *on June 28, 1936, two days before the publication of the book. Miss Gwin says, "Major Clark Howell, publisher of the paper, handed me a galley proof and said, 'Go home, read this book and write me a review for Sunday's paper.' " Like a lot of other Americans, she stayed up two nights in a row reading the book millions have not been able to put down.*

To the already distinguished list of famous writers whose works have been selected by the Book of the Month Club, Atlanta feels exceptional pride in that *Gone With the Wind* by Margaret Mitchell is the choice for July.

When H.S. Latham came "marching through Georgia," it was quite a different story from that of his predecessor, General Sherman. Both invasions, however, played major parts in carving the literary career of Miss Mitchell, brilliant young author, whose book of 1,037 pages, scheduled for publication June 30, is rich with historical events of the stirring days of the sixties.

Mr. Latham, who is vice-president of Macmillam & Company, made his visit to Georgia last spring in search of a Southern novel, embellished with the romance and tradition of the Old South and last, but not least, by a Southern writer. That Southern writer was Margaret Mitchell.

Miss Mitchell, whose work on her book has covered the better part of 10 years with never a thought of its subsequent publication, was busying herself rounding up Atlanta authors upon the request of a newspaper acquaintance who, in turn, had promised to aid Mr. Latham upon his arrival here, in search of possible book material.

It was at a tea given in his honor that he learned that the charming young Atlantan, who was dispensing Southern hospitality in all its merit

This photograph of Margaret was taken in 1936 by Kenneth Rogers.

and tradition, was an author herself, and not only was she a dyed-in-the-wool Southerner, but had written a Southern novel as well.

Arrangements were quickly made for the publishing executive to see her work. Miss Mitchell, who is imbued with an unparalleled sense of humor, laughingly recalled during her interview yesterday, that she has often wondered what Mr. Latham's reactions were, when she presented him with 60 large manila envelopes bearing the manuscript. And then later when she wired him at Charlotte, then New Orleans and then San Francisco to send it back. "I don't want to be an author," she is quoted as saying. There was no word from the publisher until he arrived in the latter city. It was from there that he wired the Atlantan of the acceptance of her book.

"It was then," said Miss Mitchell, "that I went to bed. The shock was too great. If I had any idea that my book was salable I would have stormed the markets long ago."

Margaret's girlhood home.

With the acceptance of the book, the author set about the task of checking and rechecking all the facts from four angles. Old papers, diaries, histories and biographies were consulted before she allowed the book to be published. On the Battle of Atlanta alone there were 10,000 references as to the time of day, the weather conditions, etc., of the famous conflict.

Margaret poses as a Jazz Age Flapper.   Margaret about the age of three.

As for dates and localities, Miss Mitchell found very little to alter. She wrote from knowledge of the subject. The final of the vast drama of the War Between the States was sounded long before Miss Mitchell was born. The encore lingered on, however, for history, and especially that of a Confederate nature, had been her special forte since earliest girlhood.

Her clever pen is fortified with an extensive cognition of literature and a wide vocabulary, plus an extensive clear and certain comprehension of her chosen subject.

References were for the most part on such matters as the changing mood of travel, dress and customs. For instance, up until 1890 the modern cuff links were cuff buttons. Hoopskirts, which were the vogue in 1868, were replaced by bustles, which completely transformed the female silhouette. Styles of feminine coiffure were verified as to when a headdress was a waterfall, then a chignon and then to cats, rats and mouse.

Clark Gable, Margaret and Vivien Leigh.

In the mention of travel by railroad between Chattanooga and Atlanta, Miss Mitchell was careful in checking that no mention was made of twin lines of steel prior to 1865, for it was during that year that the process of making steel was discovered.

Margaret's husband, John Marsh.

Miss Mitchell began her book in 1925, merely as a method of amuse-ment. At that time the Jazz Age was at its height. A book dealing with these customs and conventions would hardly have been appropriate, inasmuch as she herself was a part of that generation. So she turned to the sub-ject she knew — the War Between the States.

She knew Confederate history. She knew it from lengthy and extensive study and the ever-absorbing conversations with the older people. She loved knowing their customs, their pastimes and the memories of their youth. She was especially delighted of an opportunity to interview, both from the standpoint of a newspaperwoman and for personal curiosity, the last surviving members of the "thin gray line."

Three automobile accidents and sickness of members of her family over a period of seven years retarded the completion of the book. In 1929, Miss Mitchell confesses, she had written all but three chapters and she gave up, principally because she had never planned to submit it to a publisher. Until Mr. Latham came in search of talent, Miss Mitchell confides that the manuscript was a big help around the house for such necessary notations as party and grocery lists, various recipes and telephone numbers. It was well stained with coffee, too, for the author often wrote during her late breakfast hour.

A representative of distinguished and prominent forebearers, Miss Mitchell is the wife of John Marsh, a Georgia Power Company executive, to whom the book is dedicated. She is the daughter of Eugene Mitchell and the late Mrs. Maybelle Stephens Mitchell. She attended Washington Seminary in Atlanta and later Smith College, in Northampton, Massachusetts. She returned here after college days and made her debut in Atlanta society and subsequently took up newspaper work on an Atlanta paper, where she remained for several years.

Margaret and her collection of foreign editions of Gone With The Wind.

Miss Mitchell says she loathes writing and has made no plans for any future work, although she has been approached by many leading magazines.

Margaret shows indignation about men keeping their hats on in elevators.

She is a born storyteller, writing with an easy-flowing and charmingly descriptive style. Before her retirement from active newspaper work, her feature articles were outstanding and her reputation as a writer was known throughout the South. Small and dainty in stature, Miss Mitchell has made her bid for immortality by writing one of the most brilliant and greatest historical novels by an American. Copyrighted not only in America but in Canada, England and Australia as well, the publication date was delayed because of the book's selection for the Book of the Month Club.

The novel epitomizes the story of the whole South in the hard days of the War Between the States and the harder days of the Reconstruction period. It carries especial interest for Atlanta and north Georgia because it tells the story of this section as it has never been told before. By fortunate coincidence, the novel is being published when Atlanta is already making plans for celebrating its 100th anniversary, in 1937, and the vivid picture it contains of the early history of the city will stimulate pride in their city on the part of Atlantans and arouse new interest in Atlanta's dramatic past.

Scarlett O'Hara, the principal character, was the spoiled and petted darling of a wealthy planter near Atlanta, the belle of the county, interested in nothing more serious than pretty dresses and beaux, but with a will and mind of her own inherited from her father, who had come to America as an Irish immigrant and climbed upward by his own efforts.

The war brings Scarlett and Atlanta together. She arrives in 1862. She immediately felt her own kinship with the town. From then on, the reader sees Atlanta through Scarlett's eyes, through the exciting days when the South's hopes of victory were soaring high, through the period of gradually increasing hardships, and finally through the 40-day seige and the capture of the city by the Yankee army.

Scarlett had been reared to be a gentlewoman, but her gentleness dropped away and shrewdness and indomitable determination became

Margaret shown with General John M. Claypool.

ascendent under the pressure of hardships. She escapes from Atlanta on the day it is captured and makes her way laboriously through the ruined countryside to her home. She saves the home from burning when Sherman comes through on his march to the sea, and she saves it again when the Carpetbaggers try to take it away. She returns to Atlanta, and in the bitter days of the Reconstruction, slowly rebuilds her fortunes. When the book ends, the Carpetbag government has been driven out of Georgia, normal life is returning, and Scarlett has again become wealthy, but the war has taken its toll on her, just as it has with every other person in Georgia.

Paralleling Scarlett's career, but exactly opposite to her in character and temperament, is her sister-in-law, Melanie Wilkes. The two pass together from luxuries and graciousness of the antebellum civilization into the terrors of war and the horrors of Reconstruction, but Melanie is sweet and gentle in the beginning of the story and is sweet and gentle at the end. Scarlett casts away the traditions of the South and wades into her difficult situations with whatever weapon is at hand. Melanie meets the same situation, but always with good manners and grace. Melanie's courage is a thin, shining blade of steel; Scarlett's is a bludgeon.

Supplementing the picture of the effect of war on human character are the two men who loved Scarlett and Melanie. One is Ashley Wilkes, a cultured gentleman whose culture proved to be utterly worthless to him when the old civilization disappeared. The other is Rhett Butler, the outcast son of a fine Charleston family, handsome, wealthy and completely without morals or illusions.

In addition to these four, there are many other characters who fill out a cross section of Southern life: rich and poor, planters, crackers and poor whites, Carpetbaggers, scallawags, profiteers, patriots and traitors. The book is a panorama of the life in north Georgia, showing the effect of war on high and low, showing how each reacted in his own way when war crushed out the old civilization they built, and showing how they finally united in picking up the broken bits and building a new civilization with the fragments of the old.

Mrs. Marsh's theme in Gone With the Wind, is the varying effects that wars and other national catastrophes have upon people of different temperaments, and the sharply contrasting characters of Scarlett and Melanie symbolized the women who came out of the war dominating, domineering and hard, and those who retained their sweetness and charm that are traditionally associated with Southern womanhood.

Margaret with Rebecca Latimer Felton, the first woman U.S. Senator.

STEPHENS MITCHELL

In an interview with the late Stephens Mitchell, the author's brother, a few months before he died, he said:

There have been a number of streets named for Margaret and I think it's a fine tribute to her. Too many Tara's have seemed to appear all over the state. The Atlanta Library's Margaret Mitchell Room is a fine honor to her and since it is right here in Atlanta I think the rest are usless.

Many reporters have cornered me to ask if I thought a museum filled with her memorabilia would satisify me. My answer to them was a museum open to the public for free would be fine. It would be in bad taste to turn it into a commercial thing and I know Margaret would not want that.

He also said,"You knew her Yolande, and I'm sure you feel as I do that she was a fine person with many gracious habits. I'm very proud of her . She remained a lady with sweet thoughts of her many friends until the last.

Mr. Mitchell and the Trust Company of Georgia, (trustees for the Mitchell family) own the rights to Gone With The Wind.

Stephens Mitchell and Yolande Gwin.

The Postmaster General
invites you to a ceremony dedicating the
Margaret Mitchell Stamp
Omni International
Atlanta, Georgia
11:00 a.m., Monday, June 30, 1986

YOLANDE SPEAKS AT HOSPITAL

AUXILIARY MEETING

Yolande Gwin gave a talk at the September 1986 General Meeting of the Crawford Long Hospital Auxiliary. Her subject was Margaret Mitchell, *Gone With The Wind* and Yolande's forthcoming book, *I Remember Margaret Mitchell*. Photographs were taken by Jack Fleeman.

Outside the meeting room. Left to right, Shahnaz Nahai, 1987 chairman of the Ball, Anne Hamff, Yolande Gwin and Jean Chait, President of the Auxiliary.

At the luncheon. Seated left, Yolande Gwin, Jean Chait, Anne Stroud, standing left, Joyce Morgan, Anne Hamff and Matilda Pinbas.

BY THE GOVERNOR OF THE STATE OF GEORGIA

A PROCLAMATION

YOLANDE GWIN

WHEREAS: Yolande Gwin has been a society writer and editor for the Atlanta newspapers for more than 50 years; and

WHEREAS: During her many years as a journalist, Yolande Gwin has told the story of Atlanta's cultural development with delightful wit and humor; and

WHEREAS: Yolande Gwin is not only a journalists, but a historian who has written about the colorful and exciting people and events of Atlanta; and

WHEREAS   She has covered every sort of story imaginable and has interviewed celebrities ranging from Clark Gable and Vivien Leigh to J. Edgar Hoover; and

WHEREAS: Yolande Gwin wrote the first story about Margaret Mitchell's classic *Gone With The Wind* and covered the world premiere of the movie in Atlanta in 1939; and

WHEREAS: Yolande Gwin is held in the highest esteem by her peers and has been deemed the "Grande Dame of Journalism" and "the last of the great society editors;" and

WHEREAS: It is fitting that Yolande Gwin be recognized for her special journalistic talents which she has used to capture the rich heritage of our capital city and bring enjoyment to many readers; now

THEREFORE: I, Joe Frank Harris, Governor of the State of Gerogia, do hereby recognize YOLANDE GWIN as an outstanding journalist and commend her for the many contributions she has made in the field of journalism which have brought great honor to herself and to the State of Georgia.

IN WITNESS WHEREOF, I have hereunto set my hand and caused the Seal of the Executive Department to be affixed. This 1st day of December, 1983.

INDEX

CREDITS

The following individuals and organizations have granted permission
to reprint articles and photographs, for which the author is grateful.

Associated Press
Atlanta Historical Society
Atlanta Journal-Constitution, Reference Department
Atlanta Magazine, Journal-Constitution
Atlanta Junior League Magazine
Atlanta Public Library
Augusta Dearborn Edwards Archives
Brooks-Van Horne Costumes
Dekalb Historical Society
Billy Downs
Jack Fleeman
Richard Harwell Collection
Lane Brothers Photography
MacMillan Archives
Madison-Morgan Cultural Center
Metro-Goldwyn-Mayer
Stephens Mitchell Collection
Franklin Nix
Southern Travel Magazine, Atlanta Motor Club
University of Georgia Archives
Frances Marsh Zane